STORM OF ARROWS

LATE MEDIEVAL EUROPE AT WAR

Written by Richard Bodley Scott, assisted by
Nik Gaukroger, James Hamilton, Paul Robinson
and Xavier Codina

OSPREY
PUBLISHING

SLITHERINE

First published in Great Britain in 2008 by Osprey Publishing Ltd.

© 2008 Osprey Publishing Ltd and Slitherine Software UK Ltd.

Osprey Publishing, Midland House, West Way, Botley, Oxford OX2 0PH, UK
443 Park Avenue South, New York, NY 10016, USA
E-mail: info@ospreypublishing.com

Slitherine Software UK Ltd., The White Cottage, 8 West Hill Avenue, Epsom, KT 19 8LE, UK
E-mail: info@slitherine.co.uk

A CIP catalogue record for this book is available from the British Library

ISBN: 978 1 84603 345 2

Rules system written by Richard Bodley Scott, Simon Hall, and Terry Shaw
Page layout by Myriam Bell
Index by Glyn Sutcliffe
Typeset in Joanna Pro and Sleepy Hollow
Cover artwork by Peter Dennis
Photography by Duncan MacFarlane – Wargames Illustrated
Page design features supplied by istockphoto.com
All artwork and cartography © Osprey Publishing Ltd
Originated by PDQ Media, UK
Printed in China through Worldprint Ltd

08 09 10 11 12   10 9 8 7 6 5 4 3 2 1

FOR A CATALOGUE OF ALL BOOKS PUBLISHED BY OSPREY MILITARY
AND AVIATION PLEASE CONTACT:

NORTH AMERICA
Osprey Direct, c/o Random House Distribution Center, 400 Hahn Road,
Westminster, MD 21157
E-mail: info@ospreydirect.com

ALL OTHER REGIONS
Osprey Direct UK, P.O. Box 140 Wellingborough, Northants, NN8 2FA, UK
E-mail: info@ospreydirect.co.uk

Osprey Publishing is supporting the Woodland Trust, the UK's leading woodland
conservation charity, by funding the dedication of trees.

www.ospreypublishing.com
www.slitherine.com

CONTENTS

INTRODUCTION

Field of Glory is a historical miniature tabletop wargaming rules system for anyone interested in recreating the battles of the ancient and medieval eras. This companion is designed to be used alongside the *Field of Glory* rulebook and covers the armies of Western Europe from 1300 to 1500 AD.

As you look at each army, you will find the following sections:

- Brief **historical notes** on the army, its wars, its famous generals, weapons and/or troop types.
- A ready-to-play **starter army** – just put it together and play a balanced small game.
- Instructions for building a **customized army** using our points system.

- A table with the full list of **compulsory** and **optional** troops.
- Supporting **illustrations** to give you a flavour of the period.
- Miniatures photographs.

European warfare in this period was characterised by a rise in the role of infantry and a decline in the role of mounted knights. The Flemish, at Courtrai in 1302, showed that steady foot could defeat mounted knights. The Hundred Years' War, between England and France from 1337 to 1453, raged through France and spilled over into the Low Counties and Spain. The English tactical system of massed longbowmen and dismounted men-at-arms deployed in defensive positions

Ordonnance Burgundian Army deploys for battle.

4

dominated the pitched battles of the war. The French knights were themselves forced to fight on foot to stand any chance, and even then they usually lost. Nevertheless, by avoiding pitched battles and concentrating on sieges, the French eventually won the war and expelled the English from the whole of France, except for Calais.

Meanwhile, the Swiss cantons were asserting their independence from feudal rule. Their massed infantry, initially halberdiers, later mostly pikemen, trounced the Austrian chivalry on several occasions, and later smashed Charles the Bold's "perfect" Burgundian army. As the merits of the Swiss military system became apparent, pike formations were adopted in Germany and elsewhere, and

became the dominant close fighting infantry type of the early Renaissance.

The term "men-at-arms" is used in these lists to include knights and other fully equipped men-at-arms and also less well-equipped sergeants, valets, coustilliers et al, filling in rear ranks.

Equipment often varied widely in Medieval armies, even within a body of troops. Modern illustrations often show only the very best equipped men. We assume that many men, especially amongst the foot, were less well-equipped. Accordingly, we have classified troops on the basis of their probable average level of equipment.

As far as possible, we have organised the army lists into geographical groups.

The battle of Agincourt, 1415, by Gerry Embleton. Taken from Warrior 11: *English Longbowman 1330–1515.*

HUNDRED YEARS' WAR ENGLISH (CONTINENTAL)

This list covers English armies on the Continent from 1320 to 1455. This period was dominated by the Hundred Years' War between England and France. The Hundred Years' War lasted from 1337 until 1453 with intermittent pauses.

For further information on this conflict, see page 34.

THE LONGBOW

The English longbow of the Hundred Years' War period has a fearsome reputation. It was a self bow, made from imported yew by preference, about 2 metres in length. The inner side of the stave was of heartwood, which resists compression, and the outer of sapwood, which performs better in tension. Thus, although the bow was made from a single piece of wood, it used the same principle as eastern composite bows. Surviving 16th century examples from the *Mary Rose* probably had draw weights of 72–82 kgf (160–180 lbf). For comparison, a typical modern longbow has a draw weight of 27 kgf (60 lbf) or less. In order to draw such bows, archers had to train constantly from childhood. The skeletons from the *Mary Rose* testify to the extreme muscular development of the upper torso and arms required.

The main advantage of the longbow over the crossbow was a much higher rate of shooting. This allowed large bodies of archers to lay down a withering barrage of arrows against attacking enemy. Crossbows were more useful in static

English Longbows behind stakes.

situations such as sieges, where their slow rate of shooting was not an issue. The main advantage of the crossbow was that it did not require such long and athletic training to use with reasonable efficiency. At Crécy, however, the English longbowmen decisively out-shot the Genoese crossbowmen of the French.

Although the arrow storm laid down by English longbowmen was extremely effective, it was not considered enough on its own to stop a charge by mounted men-at-arms. The English invariably tried to form up in defensive positions, with their flanks secured by woods, hedges or other difficult terrain, and their front also

The Agincourt campaign, 1415. Taken from Essential Histories 19: The Hundred Years' War.

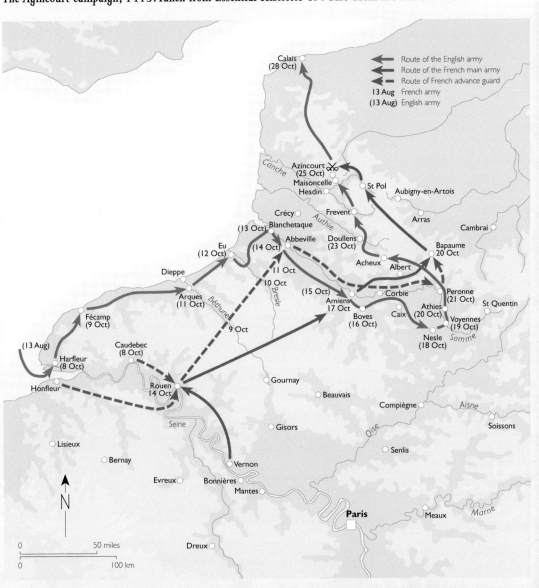

protected in one way or another. At Morlaix (1342) and Crécy (1346), for example, they formed up on a ridge behind concealed pits, at Mauron (1352) on a ridge partly protected by tangled brambles, at Poitiers (1356) behind hedges and amongst thickets and thorn bushes, at Agincourt (1415) behind muddy ploughed fields and stakes, and so on. After 1415, the use of stakes in front of the archers became standard practice, soon copied by the Burgundians and, later, by the French. At Patay (1429), however, the English archers were ridden down by mounted French men-at-arms who managed to charge them before they could emplace their stakes.

The usual formation was for the army to be divided into 2 or 3 battle groups, each consisting of a centre of dismounted men-at-arms with bodies of archers on each side.

TROOP NOTES

English and Gascon men-at-arms almost invariably fought on foot. The proportion of well-equipped men-at-arms to less well-equipped diminished as time went by, and billmen later supplemented the men-at-arms. As they fought in mixed battle groups, they are graded according to the proportion in the mix. English men-at-arms did occasionally fight mounted, though not

English Longbowmen, by Gerry Embleton. Taken from Warrior 11: English Longbowman 1330–1515.

particularly well, so count as Average when mounted. Longbowmen were armed with a variety of weapons including swords, hatchets, axes and mauls, which they were not afraid to use. We treat them as equivalent to Swordsmen. Similarly, their armour varied widely, from none at all to half-plate armour. We treat this mixture as equivalent to Protected.

HUNDRED YEARS' WAR ENGLISH (CONTINENTAL) STARTER ARMY		
Commander-in-Chief	1	Inspired Commander (Henry V)
Sub-commanders	2	2 x Troop Commander
English dismounted men-at-arms and lesser men-at-arms	3 BGs	Each comprising 4 bases of men-at-arms: Superior, Armoured, Drilled Heavy Foot – Heavy Weapon
English and Welsh longbowmen	2 BGs	Each comprising 8 bases of archers: Average, Protected, Drilled Medium Foot – Longbow, Swordsmen + Stakes (Portable Defences)
	2 BGs	Each comprising 6 bases of archers: Average, Protected, Drilled Medium Foot – Longbow, Swordsmen + Stakes (Portable Defences)
Camp	1	Unfortified camp
Total	7 BGs	Camp, 40 foot bases, 3 commanders

BUILDING A CUSTOMISED LIST USING OUR ARMY POINTS

Choose an army based on the maxima and minima in the list below. The following special instructions apply to this army:

- Commanders should be depicted as mounted or dismounted men-at-arms.
- English mounted men-at-arms can always dismount as Superior, Heavily Armoured, Drilled Heavy Foot – Heavy Weapon.
- Gascon mounted men-at-arms (whether graded as Superior or Average when mounted) can always dismount as Superior, Heavily Armoured, Undrilled Heavy Foot – Heavy Weapon.
- Hobilars can always dismount as Average, Protected, Drilled Medium Foot – Defensive spearmen.

- Dismounted men-at-arms and billmen can interpenetrate longbowmen and vice versa.
- Gascons cannot be used with German or Flemish allies. If a Flemish allied contingent is used, a German allied contingent must also be used.

Hobilar

HUNDRED YEARS' WAR ENGLISH (CONTINENTAL)

Territory Types: Agricultural, Developed, Woodlands

C-in-C		Inspired Commander/Field Commander/Troop Commander					80/50/35		1
Sub-commanders		Field Commander					50		0–2
		Troop Commander					35		0–3

Troop name	Troop Type				Capabilities		Points per base	Bases per BG	Total bases
	Type	Armour	Quality	Training	Shooting	Close Combat			
Core Troops									
English dismounted men-at-arms, lesser men-at-arms and billmen	Heavy Foot	Heavily Armoured	Superior	Drilled	–	Heavy Weapon	16	4–8	6–16
		Armoured	Superior				13		
		Armoured	Average				10		
English or Welsh longbowmen	Medium Foot	Protected	Average	Drilled	Longbow	Swordsmen	9	6–8	16–64
Stakes to cover half the bases of each longbow BG	Only from 1415	Portable defences					3		All longbow BGs or none
Optional Troops									
Mounted men-at-arms	English	Knights	Heavily Armoured	Average	Drilled	–	Swordsmen	20	4–6	0–6
	Gascon	Knights	Heavily Armoured	Superior	Undrilled	–	Lancers, Swordsmen	23	4–6	
				Average				18		
Hobilars	Only before 1350	Cavalry	Protected	Poor	Drilled	–	Swordsmen	7	4–6	0–6
Gascon dismounted men-at-arms and lesser men-at-arms		Heavy Foot	Heavily Armoured	Superior	Undrilled	–	Heavy Weapon	14	4–8	0–16
			Armoured	Superior				12		
			Armoured	Average				9		
Gascon crossbowmen		Medium Foot	Protected	Average	Undrilled	Crossbow	–	6	4–6	0–6
Gascon bidets, Irish kerns or Bretons		Light Foot	Unprotected	Average	Undrilled	Javelins	Light Spear	4	4–6	0–6
Gascon brigans		Medium Foot	Protected	Average	Undrilled	–	Swordsmen	6	4–6	0–6
Welsh spearmen	Only before 1415	Medium Foot	Unprotected	Average	Undrilled	–	Offensive Spearmen	6	6–8	0–8
German "pauncenar" spearmen	Only before 1350	Heavy Foot	Armoured	Average	Drilled	–	Defensive Spearmen	9	4	0–4
Irish horse	Only from 1415	Light Horse	Unprotected	Average	Undrilled	Javelins	Light Spear	7	4	0–4
Light guns		Light Artillery	–	Average	Undrilled	Light Artillery	–	15	2	0–2
Bombards	Only from 1415	Heavy Artillery	–	Average	Undrilled	Heavy Artillery	–	20	2	
Field fortifications		Field Fortifications						3		0–16
Fortified camp								24		0–1
Allies									
German allies (Only from 1339 to 1340) – Later Medieval German									
Flemish allies (Only in 1340) – Later Low Countries									

English men-at-arms supporting longbows.

HUNDRED YEARS' WAR ENGLISH (BRITAIN)

This list covers English armies in Britain from 1320 to 1455. Several battles were fought in this period against the Scots. The English were victorious at Dupplin Muir (1332), Halidon Hill (1333), Neville's Cross (1346) and Humbleton Hill (1402), their combination of dismounted men-at-arms and archers proving too much for the Scots schiltrons to cope with, particularly when deployed defensively. At Otterburn in 1388, a surprise night attack on the Scots by the English proved no surprise and the English were defeated. Battles were also fought between rebel and royalist forces at Boroughbridge (1322), Radcot Bridge (1387) and Shrewsbury (1403).

TROOP NOTES

Troops were raised for specific, usually short, campaigns and would not have time to come up to the drilled standard, the possible exceptions being mounted longbowmen and men-at-arms and those who had seen service in foreign wars. These could be numerous, such as the 3,000 mounted archers said to be in the army mustered before the Battle of Neville's Cross.

Men-at-arms usually fought on foot, though a small number were sometimes kept mounted. The grading of dismounted men-at-arms battle groups varies according to the proportion of well-equipped men-at-arms to lesser men-at-arms or billmen and the proportion of experienced men.

Hobilars were primarily mounted infantry, so count as Poor while mounted though they dismount as Average.

BUILDING A CUSTOMISED LIST USING OUR ARMY POINTS

Choose an army based on the maxima and minima in the list below. The following special instructions apply to this army:

- Commanders should be depicted as mounted or dismounted men-at-arms.
- Mounted men-at-arms can always dismount as Superior, Heavily Armoured, Undrilled or Drilled (as mounted type) Heavy Foot – Heavy Weapon.

- Hobilars can always dismount as Average, Protected, Undrilled or Drilled (as mounted type) Medium Foot – Defensive spearmen.
- Dismounted men-at-arms and billmen can interpenetrate longbowmen and vice versa.
- Minima marked * apply if any troops of that origin are used.
- Welsh cannot be used with Northern Border troops.

Royal standard bearer

Battle of Otterburn, 1388, by Stephen Walsh. Taken from Campaign 164: Otterburn 1388.

Battle or skirmish

English troop movements before 14 September 1402

Scottish troop movements on 14 September 1402

Road or track

0	5 miles
0	10km

N

Dunbar Castle, 7 miles

Castles of George Dunbar, Earl of March.

Cockburnspath Castle

Fast Castle

Lammermuir Hills

M A R C H

S C O T L A N D

Whiteadder Water

Duns

Combat of Nisbet, 22 June 1402
Earl of March defeats Scots.

Blackadder Water

Berwick Castle
Berwick-upon-Tweed

The Merse

Tweed

George Dunbar, Earl of March.

Norham Castle

Lindisfarne

Till

Coldstream

Wark Castle

Roxburgh Castle

Lieutenant of Roxburgh and garrison troops.

Teviot

Glen

Etal Castle

Ford Castle

N o r t h u m b e r l a n d

Milfield

English Army musters at Milfield across return route of Scots raiders.

Bamburgh and environs devastated by Earl of Douglas, October 1401.

Bamburgh Castle

Position of English Army, 14 September.

Glendale

Humbleton Hill

Wooler

Constable of Dunstanburgh rides to the muster at Milfield with his garrison.

Ralph, Baron of Greystoke with Carlisle garrison and troops from West March.

The Cheviot 2674ft

Extensively rebuilt by John of Gaunt in 1380s.

Dunstanburgh Castle

C h e v i o t   H i l l s

Earl of Northumberland and Hotspur – to Milfield.

Aln

Alnwick Castle

E N G L A N D

Garrison recently strengthened by Henry IV. Held by Sir Robert Umfraville.

Harbottle Castle

Coquet

Sir Robert and troops ride north to Milfield.

Levies from Newcastle, probably commanded by Sir Ralph Eure.

Castles of Henry Percy, Earl of Northumberland.

Warkworth Castle

Battle of Humbleton Hill, 1402. Taken from Campaign 164: Otterburn 1388.

HUNDRED YEARS' WAR ENGLISH (BRITAIN)

Territory Types: Agricultural, Hilly, Woodlands

Troop name		Type	Armour	Quality	Training	Shooting	Close Combat	Points per base	Bases per BG	Total bases	
C-in-C		Inspired Commander/Field Commander/Troop Commander						80/50/35		1	
Sub–commanders		Field Commander						50	0–2		
		Troop Commander						35	0–3		
Core Troops											
Dismounted men-at-arms, lesser men-at-arms and retinue billmen		Heavy Foot	Heavily Armoured	Superior	Undrilled	–	Heavy Weapon	14	4–8	0–16	6–16
			Heavily Armoured	Average				11			
			Armoured	Superior				12			
			Armoured	Average				9			
		Heavy Foot	Heavily Armoured	Superior	Drilled	–	Heavy Weapon	16	4–8	0–8	
			Armoured	Superior				13			
			Armoured	Average				10			
Retine and experienced longbowmen		Medium Foot	Protected	Average	Undrilled	Longbow	Swordsmen	8	6–8	0–32	12–32
		Medium Foot	Protected	Average	Drilled	Longbow	Swordsmen	9	6–8	0–16	
Optional Troops											
Mounted men-at-arms		Knights	Heavily Armoured	Average	Undrilled	–	Swordsmen	17	4–6	0–6	
		Knights	Heavily Armoured	Average	Drilled	–	Swordsmen	20	4–6		
Hobilars	Only before 1350	Cavalry	Protected	Poor	Undrilled	–	Swordsmen	6	4–6	0–6	
		Cavalry	Protected	Poor	Drilled	–	Swordsmen	7	4–6		
Town and County militia billmen		Heavy Foot	Protected	Poor	Undrilled	–	Heavy Weapon	5	4–6	0–8	
Town and County militia longbowmen		Medium Foot	Unprotected	Poor	Undrilled	Longbow	Swordsmen	5	6–8	*8–48	
			Protected					6			
Northern border horse		Light Horse or Cavalry	Protected	Average	Undrilled	–	Lancers, Swordsmen	9	4	0–4	
Northern border spearmen		Heavy Foot	Protected	Average	Undrilled	–	Defensive Spearmen	6	4–8	*4–16	
				Poor				4			
Northern border billmen		Heavy Foot	Protected	Average	Undrilled	–	Heavy Weapon	7	4	0–4	
				Poor				5			
Northern border longbowmen		Medium Foot	Unprotected	Average	Undrilled	Longbow	Swordsmen	7	4	0–4	
			Unprotected	Poor				5			
			Protected	Average				8			
			Protected	Poor				6			
Welsh longbowmen		Medium Foot	Unprotected	Average	Undrilled	Longbow	–	6	6–8	0–12	
Welsh spearmen		Medium Foot	Unprotected	Average	Undrilled	–	Offensive Spearmen	6	6–8	0–8	
Light guns		Light Artillery	–	Average	Undrilled	Light Artillery	–	15	2		
Bombards	Only from 1415	Heavy Artillery	–	Average	Undrilled	Heavy Artillery	–	20	2	0–2	
Stakes to cover half the bases of each longbow BG	Only from 1415	Portable defences						3		All longbow BGs or none	
Field fortifications		Field Fortifications						3		0–12	
Fortified camp								24		0–1	

WARS OF THE ROSES ENGLISH

This list covers English armies from the start of the Wars of the Roses in 1455 until 1500.

The Wars of the Roses were a series of conflicts between the supporters of the Lancastrian and Yorkist lines of descent from Edward III. They were characterised by bloody battles, treachery and the ruthless execution of the opposition's nobles whenever they were captured.

Footsoldiers, by Gerry Embleton. Taken from Men-at-Arms 145: The Wars of the Roses.

EDWARD IV (1442–1483)

Heir of Richard, Duke of York, Edward Earl of March succeeded to the Yorkist claim to the throne when his father was killed by the Lancastrians at the Battle of Wakefield in 1460. Despite his youth, he proved an able general, defeating the Lancastrians at Mortimer's Cross in 1461, following which he was declared king by his supporters. At Towton, later the same year, he consolidated his rule by decisively defeating the main Lancastrian army. Edward's Lancastrian cousin, King Henry VI, was deposed and fled into exile with his wife, Queen Margaret – although Henry was later captured in 1465 and imprisoned in the Tower of London. Between 1469 and 1471, Edward's principal supporter, Richard Neville "The King-Maker", Earl of Warwick, turned on him and switched to the Lancastrian side. In 1470, Edward was forced to flee to the protection of his brother-in-law Charles, Duke of Burgundy. Returning in 1471 with a small force, he rapidly raised an army and defeated and killed Warwick at Barnet. Three weeks later he defeated Queen Margaret's army at Tewkesbury. Henry VI was murdered shortly after. Edward then reigned without serious opposition until his death in 1483. He had never been defeated in battle.

TROOP NOTES

Continental mercenary troops were supplied at various times by France and Burgundy.

BUILDING A CUSTOMISED LIST USING OUR ARMY POINTS

Choose an army based on the maxima and minima in the list below. The following special instructions apply to this army:

- Commanders should be depicted as men-at-arms.

- Men-at-arms (whether graded as Superior or Average when mounted) can always dismount as Superior, Heavily Armoured, Drilled Heavy Foot – Heavy Weapon.
- Dismounted men-at-arms and billmen can interpenetrate longbowmen and vice versa.
- English allied commanders' contingents must conform to the Wars of the Roses English allies list below, but the troops in the contingent are deducted from the minima and maxima in the main list.
- Minima marked * apply if any troops of that origin are used.
- An army must be specified as Lancastrian, Yorkist, Richard III, Tudor or Yorkist Pretender (post Bosworth, 1485).
- Lancastrian armies cannot include handgunners, Bretons or pikemen.
- Yorkist armies cannot include Irish, Welsh longbowmen, Bretons, crossbowmen, nor more than the minimum sized battle group of pikemen.
- Richard III armies cannot include Irish, Welsh longbowmen, Welsh spearmen, handgunners, Bretons, crossbowmen or pikemen.
- Tudor armies cannot include Northern border troops, Irish kerns or pikemen.
- Yorkist Pretender armies cannot include Royal guard, Town and County militia, Northern border troops, Welsh longbowmen, Welsh spearmen, Bretons or crossbowmen. Yorkist Pretender armies can include up to double the normal maximum of Irish kerns.
- Town and County militia cannot be used with any Welsh or Bretons.
- Scottish allies cannot be used with any Irish or Welsh.

WARS OF THE ROSES ENGLISH

Territory Types: Agricultural, Hilly, Woodlands

C-in-C	Inspired Commander/Field Commander/Troop Commander						80/50/35	1	
Sub-commanders	Field Commander/Troop Commander						50/35	0–2	
English allied commanders	Field Commander/Troop Commander						40/25	0–2	

Troop name	Troop Type				Capabilities		Points per base	Bases per BG	Total bases
	Type	Armour	Quality	Training	Shooting	Close Combat			
Core Troops									
Dismounted men-at-arms and retinue billmen	Heavy Foot	Heavily Armoured	Superior	Drilled	–	Heavy Weapon	16	4–8	8–24
		Armoured	Superior				13		
		Armoured	Average				10		
Retinue longbowmen	Medium Foot	Protected	Average	Drilled	Longbow	Swordsmen	9	6–8	8–32
Stakes to cover half the bases of each longbow BG	Portable defences						3		All longbow BGs or none
Optional Troops									
Royal guard men-at-arms	Knights	Heavily Armoured	Superior	Drilled	–	Lancers, Swordsmen	26	2	0–2
Other mounted men-at-arms	Knights	Heavily Armoured	Average	Drilled	–	Swordsmen	20	4	0–4
Currours	Cavalry	Armoured	Average	Drilled	–	Lancers, Swordsmen	13	4	0–4
Town and County militia billmen	Heavy Foot	Protected	Poor	Undrilled	–	Heavy Weapon	5	4–6	0–12
Town and County militia longbowmen	Medium Foot	Unprotected	Poor	Undrilled	Longbow	Swordsmen	5	6–8	*6–32
		Protected					6		
Northern border horse	Light Horse or Cavalry	Protected	Average	Undrilled	–	Lancers, Swordsmen	9	4	0–4
Northern border spearmen	Heavy Foot	Protected	Average	Undrilled	–	Defensive Spearmen	6	4–8	*4–8
			Poor				4		
Northern border billmen	Heavy Foot	Protected	Average	Undrilled	–	Heavy Weapon	7	4	0–4
			Poor				5		
Northern border longbowmen	Medium Foot	Unprotected	Average	Undrilled	Longbow	Swordsmen	7	4	0–4
		Unprotected	Poor				5		
		Protected	Average				8		
		Protected	Poor				6		
Irish kerns	Medium Foot	Protected	Average	Undrilled	–	Light Spear	5	6–12	0–24
	Light Foot	Unprotected	Average	Undrilled	Javelins	Light Spear	4	6–8	
Welsh longbowmen	Medium Foot	Unprotected	Average	Undrilled	Longbow	–	6	6–8	0–12
Welsh spearmen	Medium Foot	Unprotected	Average	Undrilled	–	Offensive Spearmen	6	6–8	0–8
Mercenary handgunners	Light Foot	Unprotected	Average	Drilled	Firearm	–	4	4–6	0–6
		Protected					5		
Breton javelinmen	Light Foot	Unprotected	Average	Undrilled	Javelins	Light Spear	4	4–6	0–6
Mercenary crossbowmen	Medium Foot	Protected	Average	Drilled	Crossbow	–	7	4–8	0–8
Mercenary pikemen	Heavy Foot	Protected	Average	Drilled	–	Pikemen	6	4–12	0–16

Light guns	Light Artillery	–	Average	Undrilled	Light Artillery	–	15	2	0–2
Bombards	Heavy Artillery	–	Average	Undrilled	Heavy Artillery	–	20	2	0–2
Field fortifications	Field Fortifications						3		0–16
Fortified camp							24		0–1
Allies									
Scottish allies (Only Lancastrian armies) – Later Medieval Scots (Britain)									

WARS OF THE ROSES ENGLISH ALLIES

Allied commander	Field Commander/Troop Commander						40/25	1	
Troop name	Troop Type				Capabilities		Points per base	Bases per BG	Total bases
	Type	Armour	Quality	Training	Shooting	Close Combat			
Dismounted men-at-arms and retinue billmen	Heavy Foot	Heavily Armoured	Superior	Drilled	–	Heavy Weapon	16	4–8	4–12
		Armoured	Superior				13		
		Armoured	Average				10		
Retinue longbowmen	Medium Foot	Protected	Average	Drilled	Longbow	Swordsmen	9	6–8	6–16
Stakes to cover half the bases of each longbow BG	Portable defences						3		All longbow BGs or none

The last charge of Richard III at the battle of Bosworth, by Graham Turner. Taken from Campaign 66: Bosworth 1485.

MEDIEVAL WELSH

This list covers the army of Owain Glyndŵr (Owen Glendower) and his supporters from 1400 to 1409. During this period, Wales rebelled against English rule. The Welsh rebels captured or destroyed most of the English-held castles and lands in Wales, formed their own parliament and made alliances and treaties with foreign powers. There were several battles, most of them relatively small, but none the less significant.

They include the Battle of Bryn Glas (1402), also known as the Battle of Pilleth, where a Marcher army of around 8,000 men under Sir Edmund Mortimer was virtually annihilated by Owain's force of around 5,000. The battle began with the English army attacking up a steep slope on which the larger part of the Welsh army was deployed, suffering severely from Welsh archery as they climbed the hill. When they were fully

Owen Glendower (front) and Edward I (rear), by Christopher Rothero.
Taken from Men-at-Arms 151: The Scottish and Welsh Wars 1250–1400.

engaged, the rest of the Welsh army, which had been hidden in woods on the right flank of the English army, attacked them in flank and rear. Welsh contingents in the English army then defected, completing the English defeat. Allegedly many of the English dead were subsequently mutilated by the Welsh camp followers, in retaliation for rapes committed by English forces the previous year.

In addition, there were two major actions where Owain's forces could potentially have fought: The battle of Shrewsbury (1403) was fought before Hotspur's Welsh allies could arrive. A battle almost took place near Worcester in 1405 – Owain and his French allies stood off the royal army of Henry IV for 8 days, but no battle ultimately occurred and both sides withdrew.

TROOP NOTES

Wales was lacking in arms and armour at the beginning of the revolt. As the revolt grew, however, funds became available through raiding, and captured equipment was added to the Welsh arsenal. Most of the actions were guerrilla actions fought by highly mobile, possibly entirely mounted, bodies of troops. Where they fought on foot, hit and run attacks were the order of the day.

As the Welsh successes became known, Welshmen fighting for other nations in Europe returned to aid the rebellion. Some of these men brought their own bands of experienced soldiers with them.

Medieval Welsh Cavalryman

MEDIEVAL WELSH STARTER ARMY		
Commander-in-Chief	1	Field Commander (Owain Glyndŵr)
Sub-commanders	2	2 x Troop Commander
Followers	1 BG	4 bases of armoured followers: Superior, Armoured, Undrilled Cavalry – Lancers, Swordsmen
Raiders	1 BG	4 bases of raiders: Average, Protected, Undrilled Light Horse – Lancers, Swordsmen
Spearmen	3 BGs	Each comprising 10 bases of spearmen: Average, Unprotected, Undrilled Medium Foot – Offensive Spearmen
Experienced well-equipped longbowmen	1 BG	8 bases of longbowmen: Average, Protected, Undrilled Medium Foot – Longbow, Swordsmen
Other longbowmen	2 BGs	Each comprising 8 bases of longbowmen: Average, Unprotected, Undrilled Medium Foot – Longbow
Other longbowmen	1 BG	6 bases of longbowmen: Average, Unprotected, Undrilled Light Foot – Longbow
Camp	1	Unfortified camp
Total	9 BGs	Camp, 8 mounted bases, 60 foot bases, 3 commanders

BUILDING A CUSTOMISED LIST USING OUR ARMY POINTS

Choose an army based on the maxima and minima in the list below. The following special instructions apply to this army:

- Commanders should be depicted as mounted or dismounted followers and raiders.

- Mounted followers and raiders can always dismount as Superior or Average (as mounted type), Armoured, Protected or Unprotected (as mounted type), Undrilled Medium Foot – Heavy Weapon.
- Welsh knights cannot be used with French allies. (If French allies are used, any Welsh knights present are assumed to be included amongst the French men-at-arms.)

MEDIEVAL WELSH

Territory Types: Mountains, Hilly, Woodlands

Troop name		Troop Type				Capabilities		Points per base	Bases per BG	Total bases	
C-in-C	Inspired Commander/Field Commander/Troop Commander							80/50/35		1	
Sub-commanders	Field Commander							50		0–2	
	Troop Commander							35		0–3	
	Type	Armour	Quality	Training	Shooting	Close Combat					
Core Troops											
Followers and raiders	Cavalry	Armoured	Superior	Undrilled	–	Lancers, Swordsman		16	4–6	0–4	4–16
			Average					12			
	Cavalry	Protected	Superior	Undrilled	–	Lancers, Swordsman		12	4–6	0–12	
			Average					9			
	Light horse	Protected	Average	Undrilled	–	Lancers, Swordsman		9	4–6	0–8	
		Unprotected						8			
Welsh longbowmen	Medium Foot	Unprotected	Average	Undrilled	Longbow	–		6	6–8	0–24	8–24
	Light foot	Unprotected	Average	Undrilled	Longbow	–		6	6–8	0–12	
Welsh spearmen	Medium Foot	Unprotected	Average	Undrilled	–	Offensive Spearmen		6	6–10	16–84	24–84
	Light foot	Unprotected	Average	Undrilled	Javelins	Light spear		4	6–8	0–16	
Optional Troops											
Experienced well equipped longbowmen	Medium Foot	Protected	Average	Undrilled	Longbow	Swordsmen		8	6–8	0–12	
Welsh knights	Knights	Heavily Armoured	Average	Undrilled	–	Swordsmen		17	4	0–4	
Militia billmen	Heavy Foot	Protected	Poor	Undrilled	–	Heavy Weapon		5	4–6	0–8	
Allies											
French allies (Only in 1405) – Medieval French											

LATER MEDIEVAL SCOTS (BRITAIN)

This list covers lowland Scots armies in Britain from 1300 to 1500. Significant battles against the English during this period include victories at Loudon Hill (1307), Bannockburn (1314) and Otterburn (1388); also defeats at Dupplin Muir (1332), Halidon Hill (1333), Neville's Cross (1346) and Humbleton Hill (1402). Significant battles against Isles/Highland armies include a hard fought draw at Harlaw (1411) and a defeat at Inverlochy (1431).

Scottish raids, 1314 – 22, taken from Campaign 102: Bannockburn 1314.

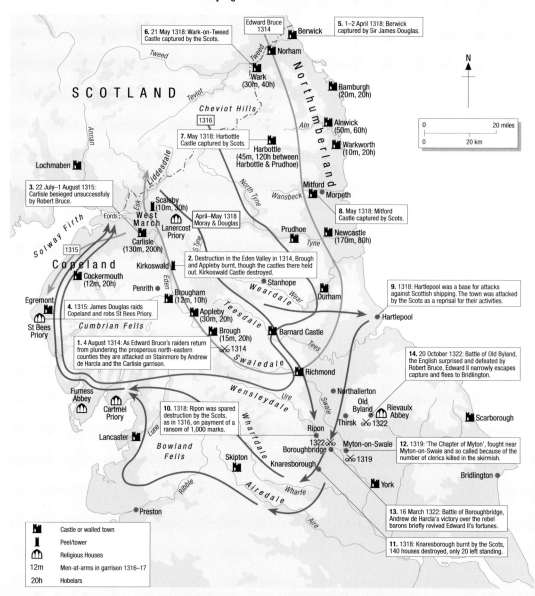

6. 21 May 1318: Wark-on-Tweed Castle captured by the Scots.

Edward Bruce 1314

5. 1–2 April 1318: Berwick captured by Sir James Douglas.

Berwick

Tweed

Norham

Wark (30m, 40h)

S C O T L A N D

Teviot

Cheviot Hills

1316

Bamburgh (20m, 20h)

Aln

Alnwick (50m, 60h)

7. May 1318: Harbottle Castle captured by Scots.

Harbottle (45m, 120h between Harbottle & Prudhoe)

Warkworth (10m, 20h)

Annan

North Tyne

Mitford

Wansbeck

Morpeth

3. 22 July–1 August 1315: Carlisle besieged unsuccessfully by Robert Bruce.

Lochmaben

Liddesdale

Scaleby (10m, 30h)

April–May 1318 Moray & Douglas

Prudhoe

Tyne

8. May 1318: Mitford Castle captured by Scots.

Newcastle (170m, 80h)

Esk

W e s t M a r c h

Fords

Lanercost Priory

Carlisle (130m, 200h)

S Tyne

2. Destruction in the Eden Valley in 1314, Brough and Appleby burnt, though the castles there held out. Kirkoswald Castle destroyed.

Kirkoswald

9. 1318: Hartlepool was a base for attacks against Scottish shipping. The town was attacked by the Scots as a reprisal for their activities.

1315

C o p e l a n d

Cockermouth (12m, 20h)

Penrith

Eden

Brougham (12m, 10h)

Stanhope

W e a r d a l e

Wear

Durham

Egremont

4. 1315: James Douglas raids Copeland and robs St Bees Priory.

T e e s d a l e

Appleby (30m, 20h)

St Bees Priory

Cumbrian Fells

Brough (15m, 20h)

1314

Barnard Castle

Hartlepool

1. 4 August 1314: As Edward Bruce's raiders return from plundering the prosperous north-eastern counties they are attacked on Stainmore by Andrew de Harcla and the Carlisle garrison.

Tees

S w a l e d a l e

Richmond

14. 20 October 1322: Battle of Old Byland, the English surprised and defeated by Robert Bruce, Edward II narrowly escapes capture and flees to Bridlington.

Furness Abbey

Cartmel Priory

W e n s l e y d a l e

Ure

Swale

Northallerton

Old Byland

Rievaulx Abbey

Scarborough

Thirsk 1322

Lancaster

Lune

10. 1318: Ripon was spared destruction by the Scots, as in 1316, on payment of a ransom of 1,000 marks.

B o w l a n d F e l l s

Wharfedale

Ripon

1322

Myton-on-Swale

Boroughbridge

1319

12. 1319: 'The Chapter of Myton', fought near Myton-on-Swale and so called because of the number of clerics killed in the skirmish.

Skipton

Knaresborough

Bridlington

Ribble

A i r e d a l e

Wharfe

York

Preston

Aire

13. 16 March 1322: Battle of Boroughbridge, Andrew de Harcla's victory over the rebel barons briefly revived Edward II's fortunes.

11. 1318: Knaresborough burnt by the Scots, 140 houses destroyed, only 20 left standing.

N o r t h u m b e r l a n d

N

0		20 miles
0	20 km	

Castle or walled town

Peel/tower

Religious Houses

12m — Men-at-arms in garrison 1316–17

20h — Hobelars

Solway Firth

TROOP NOTES

At the start of this period men-at-arms mostly fought on foot in the front ranks of the spearmen – they are assumed to be included among the spearmen. Scots contingents in France from 1418 were made up along similar lines to contemporary English armies and this appears to indicate a

Scots Spearman

change in the structure of Scots armies and an increase in the importance of archery. This can probably be dated to the years following Humbleton Hill. In France, the men-at-arms fought dismounted and we assume that they would be supported by spearmen or similar. We assume that home armies would still contain a significant number of spearmen. We can find no evidence of Scots archers using stakes. The archery reforms rapidly collapsed after the death of James I in 1437 and armies reverted to mainly spearmen.

LATER MEDIEVAL SCOTS (BRITAIN) STARTER ARMY		
Commander-in-Chief	1	Troop Commander
Sub-commanders	2	2 x Troop Commander
Men-at-arms	1 BG	4 bases of men-at-arms: Average, Heavily Armoured, Undrilled Knights – Lancers, Swordsmen
Spearmen	6 BGs	Each comprising 8 bases of spearmen: Average, Protected, Undrilled Heavy Foot – Offensive Spearmen
Archers	2 BGs	Each comprising 6 bases of archers: Average, Unprotected, Undrilled Light Foot – Longbow
Camp	1	Unfortified camp
Total	9 BGs	Camp, 4 mounted bases, 60 foot bases, 3 commanders

BUILDING A CUSTOMISED LIST USING OUR ARMY POINTS

Choose an army based on the maxima and minima in the list below. The following special instructions apply to this army:

- Commanders should be depicted as mounted or dismounted men-at-arms.
- French men-at-arms (whether graded as Superior or Average when mounted) can always dismount as Superior, Heavily Armoured, Undrilled Heavy Foot – Heavy Weapon.

Scots Ribauld

LATER MEDIEVAL SCOTS (BRITAIN)

Territory Types: Agricultural, Hilly, Woodlands

C-in-C		Inspired Commander/Field Commander/Troop Commander				80/50/35		1
Sub-commanders		Field Commander				50		0-2
		Troop Commander				35		0-3
Troop name		Troop Type				Capabilities		Points per base	Bases per BG	Total bases
		Type	Armour	Quality	Training	Shooting	Close Combat			
Core Troops										
Men-at-arms, lesser men-at-arms and retainers	Before 1403 and after 1437	Knights	Heavily Armoured	Average	Undrilled	–	Lancers, Swordsmen	18	4	0-4
	From 1403 to 1437	Heavy Foot	Heavily Armoured	Average	Undrilled	–	Heavy Weapon	11	4-8	0-8
			Armoured					9		
Spearmen		Heavy Foot	Protected	Average	Undrilled	–	Offensive Spearmen	7	6-10	32-136
Archers	Before 1403 and after 1437	Light Foot	Unprotected	Average	Undrilled	Longbow	–	6	4-8	0-12
				Poor	Undrilled	Longbow	–	4		
		Medium Foot	Unprotected	Average	Undrilled	Longbow	–	6		
				Poor	Undrilled	Longbow	–	4		
	From 1403 to 1437	Medium Foot	Protected	Average	Undrilled	Longbow	Swordsmen	8	4-8	0-16
			Protected	Poor				6		
			Unprotected	Average				7		
			Unprotected	Poor				5		
Optional Troops										
Ribaulds		Medium Foot	Unprotected	Poor	Undrilled	–	–	2	6	0-6
Light guns	Only from 1339	Light Artillery	–	Average	Undrilled	Light Artillery	–	15	2	0-2
Bombards	Only from 1339	Heavy Artillery	–	Average	Undrilled	Heavy Artillery	–	20	2	0-2
Pits or other traps		Field Fortifications						3		0-16
Fortified camp								24		0-1
Allies										
Isles and/or Highland allies – Later Scots Isles and Highlands										
Special Campaigns										
Only in 1385										
French men-at-arms		Knights	Superior	Undrilled	Heavily Armoured	–	Lancers, Swordsmen	23	4	4
			Average					18		
French crossbowmen		Medium Foot	Average	Undrilled	Protected	Crossbow	–	6	4	0-4

LATER MEDIEVAL SCOTS ALLIES (BRITAIN)

Allied commander		Field Commander/Troop Commander				40/25		1
Troop name		Troop Type				Capabilities		Points per base	Bases per BG	Total bases
		Type	Armour	Quality	Training	Shooting	Close Combat			
Spearmen		Heavy Foot	Protected	Average	Undrilled	–	Offensive Spearmen	7	6-10	12-32

LATER MEDIEVAL SCOTS (CONTINENTAL)

This list covers the Scottish mercenary armies operating in France and Burgundy from 1418 to 1429.

TROOP NOTES

Records show that unlike Scottish "home" armies these contingents were made up along the lines of contemporary English armies with archers outnumbering men-at-arms by 2:1. Fighting was undertaken on foot. The option for Armoured men-at-arms allows for the possibility that their numbers were made up by a significant number of lesser men-at-arms and spearmen in incomplete harness. Discipline in Scots contingents appears to have been variable.

The maxima of this list assume that large armies will include a French allied contingent.

French allied troops, by Christopher Rothero.
Taken from Men-at-Arms 151: The Scottish and Welsh Wars 1250–1400.

BUILDING A CUSTOMISED LIST USING OUR ARMY POINTS

Choose an army based on the maxima and minima in the list below. The following special instructions apply to this army:

- Commanders should be depicted as men-at-arms.

Bombard

LATER MEDIEVAL SCOTS (CONTINENTAL)

Territory Types: Agricultural, Developed, Woodlands

Troop name	Troop Type				Capabilities		Points per base	Bases per BG	Total bases
C-in-C	Inspired Commander/Field Commander/Troop Commander						80/50/35		1
Sub-commanders	Field Commander						50		0–2
	Troop Commander						35		0–3
	Type	Armour	Quality	Training	Shooting	Close Combat			
Core Troops									
Men-at-arms, lesser men-at-arms and retainers	Heavy Foot	Heavily Armoured	Average	Undrilled	–	Heavy Weapon	11	4–8	8–32
		Armoured					9		
Archers	Medium Foot	Protected	Average	Undrilled	Longbow	Swordsmen	8	4–8	16–64
		Protected	Poor				6		
		Unprotected	Average				7		
		Unprotected	Poor				5		
Optional Troops									
Ribaulds	Medium Foot	Unprotected	Poor	Undrilled	–	–	2	6	0–6
Light guns	Light Artillery	–	Average	Undrilled	Light Artillery	–	15	2	0–2
Bombards	Heavy Artillery	–	Average	Undrilled	Heavy Artillery	–	20	2	
Pits or other traps	Field Fortifications						3		0–16
Fortified camp							24		0–1
Allies									
French Allies – Medieval French									

LATER MEDIEVAL SCOTS (CONTINENTAL) ALLIES

Troop name	Troop Type				Capabilities		Points per base	Bases per BG	Total bases
Allied commander	Field Commander/Troop Commander						40/25		1
	Type	Armour	Quality	Training	Shooting	Close Combat			
Men-at-arms, lesser men-at-arms and retainers	Heavy Foot	Heavily Armoured	Average	Undrilled	–	Heavy Weapon	11	4–8	4–8
		Armoured					9		
Archers	Medium Foot	Protected	Average	Undrilled	Longbow	Swordsmen	8	4–8	8–16
		Protected	Poor				6		
		Unprotected	Average				7		
		Unprotected	Poor				5		

LATER SCOTS ISLES AND HIGHLANDS

This list covers the armies of the Lordship of the Isles from 1300 until 1493 when the last Lord was executed.

TROOP NOTES

The commonest weapon of the Islesman was the two-handed axe, but some Isles and most West Highlands grave effigies show spear and sword instead. Battle accounts from this period and later suggest that the wealthier Highlanders were equipped with mail, bow, targe, sword and/or axe. Lesser followers, equipped only with targe, sword or knife made up the rear ranks.

Ilsesman

LATER SCOTS ISLES AND HIGHLANDS STARTER ARMY		
Commander-in-Chief	1	Field Commander
Sub-commanders	2	2 x Troop Commander
Islesmen	5 BGs	Each comprising 8 bases of Islesmen: Average, Protected, Undrilled Heavy Foot – Heavy Weapon
Highlanders	4 BGs	Each comprising 6 bases of Highlanders: Average, Protected, Undrilled Medium Foot – Bow*, Impact Foot, Swordsmen
Camp	1	Unfortified camp
Total	9 BGs	Camp, 64 foot bases, 3 commanders

BUILDING A CUSTOMISED LIST USING OUR ARMY POINTS

Choose an army based on the maxima and minima in the list below. The following special instructions apply to this army:

- Commanders should be depicted as Islesmen or Highlanders.

Highlander

LATER SCOTS ISLES AND HIGHLANDS									
Territory Types: Hilly, Mountains									
C-in-C	Inspired Commander/Field Commander/Troop Commander						80/50/35	1	
Sub-commanders	Field Commander						50	0–2	
	Troop Commander						35	0–3	
Troop name	Troop Type				Capabilities		Points per base	Bases per BG	Total bases
	Type	Armour	Quality	Training	Shooting	Close Combat			
Core Troops									
Islesmen	Heavy Foot	Protected	Average	Undrilled	–	Heavy Weapon	7	6–8	32–100
	Heavy Foot	Protected	Average	Undrilled	–	Offensive Spearmen	7	6–8	
Highlanders	Medium Foot	Protected	Average	Undrilled	Bow*	Impact Foot, Swordsmen	8	6–8	0–48
Scouts	Light Foot	Unprotected	Average	Undrilled	Bow	–	5	4	0–4

LATER SCOTS ISLES AND HIGHLANDS ALLIES

Allied commander	Field Commander/Troop Commander					40/25	1	
Troop name	Troop Type				Capabilities		Points per base	Bases per BG	Total bases
	Type	Armour	Quality	Training	Shooting	Close Combat			
Islesmen	Heavy Foot	Protected	Average	Undrilled	–	Heavy Weapon	7	6–8	0–16
	Heavy Foot	Protected	Average	Undrilled	–	Offensive Spearmen	7	6–8	
Highlanders	Medium Foot	Protected	Average	Undrilled	Bow*	Impact Foot, Swordsmen	8	6–8	0–16

LATER ANGLO-IRISH

This list covers Anglo-Irish armies from 1300 to 1500. The title of the English governor changed over the period from Justiciar to Lieutenant and then to Lord Deputy. For convenience he will be referred to hereafter as the Justiciar.

TROOP NOTES

Justiciar's hobilars were primarily mounted infantry, so count as Poor while mounted.

*Justiciar's
man-at-arms*

LATER ANGLO-IRISH STARTER ARMY

Commander-in-Chief	1	Field Commander
Sub-commanders	2	2 x Troop Commander
Justiciar's men-at-arms	1 BG	4 bases of men-at-arms: Average, Heavily Armoured, Drilled Knights – Lancers, Swordsmen
Justiciar's longbowmen	1 BG	6 bases of longbowmen: Average, Protected, Drilled Medium Foot – Longbow, Swordsmen
Anglo-Irish spears	1 BG	4 bases of Anglo-Irish spears: Superior, Armoured, Undrilled Cavalry – Light Spear, Swordsmen
Irish horse	1 BG	6 bases of Irish horse: Average, Unprotected, Undrilled Light Horse – Javelins, Light Spear
Galloglaigh	2 BGs	Each comprising 6 bases of galloglaigh: Superior, Protected, Undrilled Heavy Foot – Heavy Weapon
Colonist longbowmen	2 BGs	Each comprising 6 bases of longbowmen: Average, Protected, Undrilled Medium Foot – Longbow, Swordsmen
Irish kerns	2 BGs	Each comprising 6 bases of kerns: Poor, Unprotected, Undrilled Light Foot – Javelins, Light Spear
Camp	1	Unfortified camp
Total	10 BGs	Camp, 14 mounted bases, 42 foot bases, 3 commanders

BUILDING A CUSTOMISED LIST USING OUR ARMY POINTS

Choose an army based on the maxima and minima in the list below. The following special instructions apply to this army:

- The Justiciar should be depicted as men-at-arms.
- Anglo-Irish commanders should be depicted as Anglo-Irish lances or spears.
- Justiciar's men-at-arms can always dismount as Superior, Heavily Armoured, Drilled Heavy Foot – Heavy Weapon.
- Justiciar's hobilars can always dismount as Average, Protected, Drilled Medium Foot – Defensive spearmen.
- Troops marked * can only be used if the Justiciar is the C-in-C. The minimum marked * applies only if any troops so marked are used.
- Dismounted men-at-arms and billmen can interpenetrate longbowmen and vice versa.
- Anglo-Irish allied commanders' contingents must conform to the Anglo-Irish allies list below, but the troops in the contingent are deducted from the minima and maxima in the main list.

Anglo-Irish troops, by David Sque. Taken from Men-at-Arms 256: The Irish Wars 1485–1603.

LATER ANGLO-IRISH

Territory Types: Agricultural

C-in-C (Justiciar or Anglo-Irish)	Inspired Commander/Field Commander/Troop Commander					80/50/35		1	
Anglo-Irish sub-commanders	Field Commander/Troop Commander					50/35		0–2	
Anglo-Irish allied commanders	Field Commander/Troop Commander					40/25		0–2	

Troop name		Troop Type				Capabilities		Points per base	Bases per BG	Total bases	
		Type	Armour	Quality	Training	Shooting	Close Combat				
Core Troops											
Justiciar's men-at-arms		Knights	Heavily Armoured	Average	Drilled	–	Lancers, Swordsmen	21	4	*0–4	
		Knights	Heavily Armoured	Average	Drilled	–	Swordsmen	20			
Justiciar's hobilars	Only before 1400	Cavalry	Protected	Poor	Drilled	–	Swordsmen	7	4	*0–4	
Justiciar's longbowmen		Medium Foot	Protected	Average	Drilled	Longbow	Swordsmen	9	4–6	*4–6	
Anglo–Irish lances		Cavalry	Armoured	Superior	Undrilled	–	Lancers, Swordsmen	16	4–6	0–6	4–12
Anglo–Irish spears		Cavalry	Armoured	Superior	Undrilled	–	Light Spear, Swordsmen	16	4–6	4–12	
Irish horse		Light Horse	Unprotected	Average	Undrilled	Javelins	Light Spear	7	4–6	0–6	
Colonist longbowmen	Before 1400	Medium Foot	Unprotected	Average	Undrilled	Longbow	Swordsmen	7	6–8	0–18	12–30
			Protected					8			
		Medium Foot	Unprotected	Poor	Undrilled	Longbow	Swordsmen	5	6–8	0–30	
			Protected					6			
	From 1400	Medium Foot	Unprotected	Average	Undrilled	Longbow	Swordsmen	7	6–8	6–12	
			Protected					8			
		Medium Foot	Unprotected	Poor	Undrilled	Longbow	Swordsmen	5	6–8		
			Protected					6			
Colonist billmen	Only from 1400	Heavy Foot	Protected	Average	Undrilled	–	Heavy Weapon	7	6–8	0–12	8–24
		Heavy Foot	Protected	Poor	Undrilled	–	Heavy Weapon	5	6–8	0–24	
Galloglaigh		Heavy Foot	Protected	Superior	Undrilled	–3	Heavy Weapon	9	6–8	0–18	
				Average				7			
Irish kerns		Medium Foot	Protected	Average	Undrilled	–	Light Spear	5	6–12	12–60	
		Light Foot	Unprotected	Average	Undrilled	Javelins	Light Spear	4	6–8		
				Poor				2			
Optional Troops											
Irish archers		Light Foot	Unprotected	Average	Undrilled	Bow	–	5	4	0–4	
Bombards	Only from 1400	Heavy Artillery	–	Average	Undrilled	Heavy Artillery	–	20	2	*0–2	
Stakes to cover half the bases of each longbow BG	Only from 1415	Portable defences						3		All or none	
Fortified camp								24		0–1	
Allies											
Irish allies											

LATER ANGLO-IRISH ALLIES

Anglo–Irish allied commander		Field Commander/Troop Commander						40/25		1	
Troop name		Troop Type				Capabilities		Points per base	Bases per BG	Total bases	
		Type	Armour	Quality	Training	Shooting	Close Combat				
Anglo–Irish spears		Cavalry	Armoured	Superior	Undrilled	–	Light Spear, Swordsmen	16	4	0–4	
Colonist longbowmen		Medium Foot	Unprotected	Average	Undrilled	Longbow	Swordsmen	7	4–8	0–8	4–12
			Unprotected	Poor				5			
			Protected	Average				8			
			Protected	Poor				6			
Colonist billmen	Only from 1400	Heavy Foot	Protected	Average	Undrilled	–	Heavy Weapon	7	4–8	4–8	
				Poor				5			
Stakes to cover half the bases of each longbow BG	Only from 1415	Portable defences						3		All or none	
Galloglaigh		Heavy Foot	Protected	Superior	Undrilled	–	Heavy Weapon	9	4–6	0–6	
				Average				7			
Irish kerns		Medium Foot	Protected	Average	Undrilled	–	Light Spear	5	6–8	0–16	
		Light Foot	Unprotected	Average	Undrilled	Javelins	Light Spear	4	4–6		
				Poor				2			

MEDIEVAL IRISH

This list covers Irish armies from 1300 to 1500.

GALLOGLAIGH

Galloglaigh (foreign warriors), or "galloglasses" as they were also known, were originally mercenary warriors from the Western Isles and west coast of Scotland, serving under their own chieftains. Several clans of galloglaigh settled permanently in Ireland, notably the MacSúibhne (MacSweeney), MacDomhnaill (MacDonnell/MacDowell), MacSíothaigh (MacSheehy), MacDubhgaill (MacDougall), MacCaba (MacCabe) and MacRuari (MacRory) clans. They were employed both by the Irish and the Anglo-Irish. By the 15th century, galloglaigh came to include native Irishmen.

As solid infantry, with a reputation for steadiness, galloglaigh were at the forefront of the Irish revival in the 15th century, allowing the Irish to match the heavier troops of the Anglo-Irish. They became the mainstay of Irish warfare, supported by mounted nobles and lightly equipped kerns.

The principle galloglaigh weapon was the two-handed axe, though not all were so armed. They aspired to a mail coat, but grave effigies make it clear that a high proportion wore only a helmet and the textile cotun (akheton).

Irish Kern

MEDIEVAL IRISH STARTER ARMY

Commander-in-Chief	1	Field Commander
Sub-commanders	2	2 x Troop Commander
Armoured cavalry	1 BG	4 bases of armoured cavalry: Superior, Armoured, Undrilled Cavalry – Light Spear, Swordsmen
Light horse	2 BGs	Each comprising 4 bases of light horse: Average, Unprotected, Undrilled Light Horse – Javelins, Light Spear
Galloglaigh	4 BGs	Each comprising 6 bases of galloglaigh: Superior, Protected, Undrilled Heavy Foot – Heavy Weapon
Kerns	2 BGs	Each comprising 8 bases of kerns: Average, Protected, Undrilled Medium Foot – Light Spear
Kerns	2 BGs	Each comprising 8 bases of kerns: Average, Unprotected, Undrilled Light Foot – Javelins, Light Spear
Camp	1	Unfortified camp
Total	11 BGs	Camp, 12 mounted bases, 56 foot bases, 3 commanders

Galloglaighs, by David Sque. Taken from Men-at-Arms 256: The Irish Wars 1485–1603.

BUILDING A CUSTOMISED LIST USING OUR ARMY POINTS

Choose an army based on the maxima and minima in the list below. The following special instructions apply to this army:

- Irish commanders should be depicted as armoured cavalry or light horse.

- Edward Bruce should be depicted as Scottish men-at-arms.

- Irish allied commanders' contingents must conform to the Irish allies list below, but the troops in the contingent are deducted from the minima and maxima in the main list.

- Plashed wood edges can only be used in plantations or forest.

MEDIEVAL IRISH

Territory Types: Agricultural, Hilly, Woodlands

Irish C-in-C	Inspired Commander/Field Commander/Troop Commander						80/50/35	1	
Irish sub-commanders	Field Commander/Troop Commander						50/35	0–2	
Irish allied commanders	Field Commander/Troop Commander						40/25	0–2	

Troop name	Troop Type				Capabilities		Points per base	Bases per BG	Total bases
	Type	Armour	Quality	Training	Shooting	Close Combat			
Core Troops									
Armoured cavalry	Cavalry	Armoured	Superior	Undrilled	–	Lancers, Swordsmen	16	4	0–4
	Cavalry	Armoured	Superior	Undrilled	–	Light Spear, Swordsmen	16		
Light horse	Light Horse	Unprotected	Average	Undrilled	Javelins	Light Spear	7	4–6	4–10
Galloglaigh	Heavy Foot	Protected	Superior	Undrilled	–	Heavy Weapon	9	6–8	8–30
			Average				7		
Kerns	Medium Foot	Protected	Average	Undrilled	–	Light Spear	5	6–12	32–160
	Light Foot	Unprotected	Average	Undrilled	Javelins	Light Spear	4	6–8	
			Poor				2		
Optional Troops									
Rising Out	Mob	Unprotected	Poor	Undrilled	–	–	2	8–12	0–12
Archers	Light Foot	Unprotected	Average	Undrilled	Bow	–	5	6–8	0–12
Plashed wood edges	Field Fortifications						3		0–12
Allies									
Anglo–Irish allies									
Special Campaigns									
Edward Bruce's campaign from 1315 to 1318									
Replace Irish C–in–C with Scottish C–in–C (Edward Bruce)	Field Commander/Troop Commander						50/35	1	
Scottish men-at-arms	Knights	Heavily Armoured	Average	Undrilled	–	Lancers, Swordsmen	18	4	0–4
Scottish spearmen	Heavy Foot	Protected	Average	Undrilled	–	Offensive Spearmen	7	6–10	8–12

MEDIEVAL IRISH ALLIES									
Allied commander	Field Commander/Troop Commander						40/25		1
Troop name	Troop Type				Capabilities		Points per base	Bases per BG	Total bases
	Type	Armour	Quality	Training	Shooting	Close Combat			
Light horse	Light Horse	Unprotected	Average	Undrilled	Javelins	Light Spear	7	4	0–4
Galloglaigh	Heavy Foot	Protected	Superior	Undrilled	–	Heavy Weapon	9	4–8	4–8
			Average				7		
Kerns	Medium Foot	Protected	Average	Undrilled	–	Light Spear	5	6–12	8–36
	Light Foot	Unprotected	Average	Undrilled	Javelins	Light Spear	4	6–8	
			Poor				2		

MEDIEVAL FRENCH

This list covers French armies from 1300 until the Ordonnance reforms of 1445.

THE HUNDRED YEARS' WAR

The period was dominated by the Hundred Years' War between England and France. The Hundred Years' War lasted from 1337 to 1453 with intermittent pauses. At the height of Angevin power, in the late 12th century, the King of England ruled larger territories in France than the King of France himself, including Normandy, Maine, Anjou, Touraine, Gascony, Saintonge and Aquitaine. By the start of the Hundred Years' War, however, English possessions had been reduced to Gascony, with its capital at Bordeaux. When Charles IV of France died in 1328, leaving only a daughter, King Edward III of England was, in fact, his closest living male relative. By English law, this made him heir to the throne of France. The French nobility, however, could not face the prospect of an English king, and invoked the ancient Salic law by which the royal inheritance of France could not pass through a woman. They therefore declared Philip of Valois, the nearest relative in the male line, to be the heir to the throne, and crowned him king as Philip VI. In 1331, Edward gave up his claim to the

French throne in return for confirmation of his possession of Gascony. In 1337, however, Philip declared Gascony forfeit, and Edward, in response, reasserted his claim to the French throne and declared war.

The first phase of the war lasted from 1337 to 1360. During this period the French countryside was devastated and the English won a series of victories against French armies. Having proved at Crécy in 1346 that their mounted knights could not prevail against the English combination of longbowmen and dismounted men-at-arms deployed in a defensive position, the French began to dismount most of their knights to fight on foot. At Poitiers, in 1356, the French main battle fought on foot. However, the English were deployed behind hedges amongst thickets and scrub, and the battle once again ended in disaster for the French. In 1360, the Treaty of Brétigny was signed. By the terms of this, Edward once again renounced his claim to the throne of France, but the English held Aquitaine, Calais, Ponthieu and half of Brittany.

In the second phase of the war, from 1369, the English were progressively pushed back until a truce was signed in 1389.

French cavalry, by Angus McBride. Taken from Men-at-Arms 337: French Armies of the Hundred Years' War.

In 1415, Henry V of England once again declared war. At the battle of Agincourt, the same year, the French were once again defeated. This time the English formed up in muddy ploughed fields, and also used a barricade of 2 metre (6 foot) sharpened stakes in front of their archers. The initial mounted French attacks were repulsed with heavy losses, and the main attack by dismounted men-at-arms also met with disaster. By the resulting Treaty of Troyes, Henry held most of northern France and was recognised as the heir to the French throne, the dauphin (later Charles VII) being declared illegitimate. Needless to say, Charles did not agree to this and continued the fight.

Henry died in 1422 while still in France, and was succeeded by his infant son Henry VI. English fortunes continued to be good, however, until 1429, when the French, inspired by Joan of Arc, forced the English to lift the siege of Orleans. Shortly afterwards they defeated another English army at Patay. A mounted French charge contacted the English archers before they could emplace their stakes and rode them down. Despite the capture and execution of Joan of Arc the following year, French fortunes continued to improve. By avoiding open battle, the French were able to gradually retake their towns one by one. After the defeat of Castillon in 1453, the English were left holding only the area immediately around Calais.

French defend the city approaches.

TROOP NOTES

There is a school of thought that once French men-at-arms became used to fighting on foot, they lost much of their élan when mounted. We therefore allow the option to grade them as Average when mounted – they are still Superior when dismounted. Brigans were lightly armed infantry equipped with a variety of weapons. Ribauds and pillards were armed principally with knives and were fit only for slaying unhorsed enemy men-at-arms.

MEDIEVAL FRENCH STARTER ARMY		
Commander-in-Chief	1	Troop Commander
Sub-commanders	2	2 x Troop Commander
Men-at-arms	3 BGs	Each comprising 4 bases of men-at-arms: Superior, Heavily Armoured, Undrilled Knights – Lancers, Swordsmen
Genoese crossbowmen	1 BG	6 bases of crossbowmen: Average, Protected, Drilled Medium Foot – Crossbow
French crossbowmen	2 BGs	Each comprising 6 bases of crossbowmen: Average, Protected, Undrilled Medium Foot – Crossbow
Voulgiers	1 BG	8 bases of voulgiers: Average, Armoured, Drilled Heavy Foot – Heavy Weapon
Peasant levies	1 BG	8 bases of peasants: Poor, Unprotected, Undrilled Mob – no capabilities
Camp	1	Unfortified camp
Total	8 BGs	Camp, 12 mounted bases, 34 foot bases, 3 commanders

French infantry, by Angus McBride. Taken from Men-at-Arms 337: French Armies of the Hundred Years' War.

BUILDING A CUSTOMISED LIST USING OUR ARMY POINTS

Choose an army based on the maxima and minima in the list below. The following special instructions apply to this army:

- Commanders should be depicted as men-at-arms.

- French men-at-arms (whether graded as Superior or Average when mounted) can always dismount as Superior, Heavily Armoured, Undrilled Heavy Foot – Heavy Weapon.
- Mercenary men-at-arms can always dismount as Average, Heavily Armoured, Drilled Heavy Foot – Heavy Weapon.

French men-at-arms charge!

MEDIEVAL FRENCH

Territory Types: Agricultural, Developed, Woodlands

C-in-C		Inspired Commander/Field Commander/Troop Commander				80/50/35		1	
Sub-commanders		Field Commander				50		0–2	
		Troop Commander				35		0–3	

Troop name		Troop Type				Capabilities		Points per base	Bases per BG	Total bases
		Type	Armour	Quality	Training	Shooting	Close Combat			
Core Troops										
French men-at-arms	Any date	Knights	Heavily Armoured	Superior	Undrilled	–	Lancers, Swordsmen	23	4–6	8–30
	Only from 1350	Knights	Heavily Armoured	Average	Undrilled	–	Lancers, Swordsmen	18	4–6	
French crossbowmen		Medium Foot	Protected	Average	Undrilled	Crossbow	–	6	6–8	6–16
		Medium Foot	Protected	Poor	Drilled	Crossbow	–	5	6–8	
Brigans		Medium Foot	Protected	Average	Undrilled	–	Swordsmen	6	6–8	6–12
Ribauds, pillards and peasant levies		Mob	Unprotected	Poor	Undrilled	–	–	2	8–12	
Optional Troops										
Separately deployed valets de guerre	Only from 1400	Cavalry	Armoured	Average	Undrilled	–	Lancers, Swordsmen	12	4–6	0–6
Mercenary men-at-arms		Knights	Heavily Armoured	Average	Drilled	–	Lancers, Swordsmen	21	4	0–4
Genoese crossbowmen		Medium Foot	Protected	Average	Drilled	Crossbow	–	7	6–8	0–12
Spanish crossbowmen		Light Foot	Unprotected	Average	Undrilled	Crossbow	–	5	4–6	0–6
French archers		Medium Foot	Unprotected	Poor	Undrilled	Longbow	–	4	4	0–4
Bidets	Only before 1400	Light Foot	Unprotected	Average	Undrilled	Javelins	Light Spear	4	4–6	0–6
Pavisiers	Only from 1350 to 1399	Heavy Foot	Heavily Armoured	Average	Drilled	–	Defensive Spearmen	12	6–8	0–8
			Armoured					9		
Voulgiers	Only from 1400	Heavy Foot	Armoured	Average	Drilled	–	Heavy Weapon	10	6–8	
Light guns	Only from 1350	Light Artillery	–	Average	Undrilled	Light Artillery	–	15	2	0–2
Heavy guns	Only from 1350	Heavy Artillery	–	Average	Undrilled	Heavy Artillery	–	20	2	0–2
Fortified camp								24		0–1
Allies										
Scottish allies (Only from 1418 to 1429) – Later Medieval Scots (Continental)										

MEDIEVAL FRENCH ALLIES

Allied commander		Field Commander/Troop Commander						40/25		1	
Troop name		Troop Type				Capabilities		Points per base	Bases per BG	Total bases	
		Type	Armour	Quality	Training	Shooting	Close Combat				
Men-at-arms	Any date	Knights	Heavily Armoured	Superior	Undrilled	–	Lancers, Swordsmen	23	4–6	4–8	
	Only from 1350	Knights	Heavily Armoured	Average	Undrilled	–	Lancers, Swordsmen	18	4–6		
French crossbowmen		Medium Foot	Protected	Average	Undrilled	Crossbow	–	6	4–6	4–6	
		Medium Foot	Protected	Poor	Drilled	Crossbow	–	5	4–6		

ORDONNANCE FRENCH

This list covers French armies from the Ordonnance reforms of 1445 until 1500.

TROOP NOTES

The Ordonnance of 1445 decreed the raising of 15 ordonnance companies, each consisting of 100 lances. Each lance consisted of 6 mounted men, comprising a man-at-arms, a coustillier, a page and, depending on which source is believed, either 3 archers or 2 archers and a valet de guerre.

Coustilliers were somewhat more lightly equipped cavalry that filled the rear ranks behind the men-at-arms, so are included amongst the men-at-arms, as are valets de guerre. The archers normally rode to battle, but fought on foot. Later in the period, however, they sometimes operated as lance armed cavalry, so can be fielded as such from 1466. From 1480, the Kings of France regularly employed Swiss mercenaries, numbering around 6,000 throughout the remainder of Louis XI's reign.

ORDONNANCE FRENCH STARTER ARMY		
Commander-in-Chief	1	Field Commander
Sub-commanders	2	2 x Troop Commander
Ordonnance men-at-arms	2 BGs	Each comprising 4 bases of men-at-arms: Superior, Heavily Armoured, Drilled Knights – Lancers, Swordsmen
Ordonnance longbowmen	2 BGs	Each comprising 6 bases of longbowmen: Average, Protected, Drilled Medium Foot – Longbow, Swordsmen
Swiss pikemen	1 BG	8 bases of Swiss pikemen: Superior, Protected, Drilled Heavy Foot – Pikemen
Polearmsmen	2 BGs	Each comprising 4 bases of polearmsmen: Average, Armoured, Undrilled Heavy Foot – Heavy Weapon
Francs archers	1 BG	6 bases of longbowmen: Poor, Unprotected, Undrilled Medium Foot – Longbow
Camp	1	Unfortified camp
Total	8 BGs	Camp, 8 mounted bases, 34 foot bases, 3 commanders

BUILDING A CUSTOMISED LIST USING OUR ARMY POINTS

Choose an army based on the maxima and minima in the list below. The following special instructions apply to this army:

- Commanders should be depicted as men-at-arms.
- Ordonnance men-at-arms can always dismount before 1466 as Superior, Heavily Armoured, Drilled Heavy Foot – Heavy Weapon.
- Feudal men-at-arms (whether graded as Superior or Average when mounted) can always dismount before 1466 as Superior, Heavily Armoured, Undrilled Heavy Foot – Heavy Weapon.
- Italian men-at-arms can always dismount before 1466 as Average, Heavily Armoured, Drilled Heavy Foot – Heavy Weapon.
- Ordonnance longbowmen upgraded to cavalry can always dismount as Average, Protected, Drilled Medium Foot – Longbow, Swordsmen, without stakes.
- The minimum marked * applies if any Swiss are used.

ORDONNANCE FRENCH

Territory Types: Agricultural, Developed, Woodlands

C-in-C	Inspired Commander/Field Commander/Troop Commander						80/50/35		1	
Sub-commanders	Field Commander						50		0–2	
	Troop Commander						35		0–3	

Troop name	Troop Type				Capabilities		Points per base	Bases per BG	Total bases	
	Type	Armour	Quality	Training	Shooting	Close Combat				
Core Troops										
Ordonnance men-at-arms	Knights	Heavily Armoured	Superior	Drilled	–	Lancers, Swordsmen	26	4–6	6–18	
Ordonnance longbowmen	Medium Foot	Protected	Average	Drilled	Longbow	Swordsmen	9	6–8	6–18	
Stakes to cover half the bases of each non-upgraded Ordonnance longbow BG	Portable defences						3	All non–upgraded Ordonnance longbow BGs or none		
Upgrade longbowmen to cavalry	Only from 1466	Cavalry	Protected	Average	Drilled		Lancers, Swordsmen	10	4–6	0–6
Francs archers	Medium Foot	Unprotected	Poor	Undrilled	Longbow	–	4	6–8	6–18	
Optional Troops										
Polearmsmen	Heavy Foot	Armoured	Average	Undrilled	–	Heavy Weapon	9	4–8	0–8	
	Heavy Foot	Armoured	Poor	Drilled	–	Heavy Weapon	8	4–8		
Spearmen	Only before 1466	Heavy Foot	Protected	Poor	Drilled	–	Defensive Spearmen	5	4–8	0–8
					Undrilled			4		
French pikemen and halberdiers	Only from 1466	Heavy Foot	Protected	Poor	Drilled		Pikemen	4	8–12	0–12
Crossbowmen	Medium Foot	Protected	Average	Undrilled	Crossbow	–	6	6–8	0–16	
	Medium Foot	Protected	Poor	Drilled	Crossbow	–	5	6–8	0–16	
	Medium Foot	Protected	Average	Drilled	Crossbow	–	7	6–8	0–8	
	Light Foot	Unprotected	Average	Undrilled	Crossbow	–	5	4	0–4	
Handgunners	Light Foot	Unprotected	Average	Drilled	Firearm	–	4	4	0–4	
		Protected					5			
Bidets	Light Foot	Unprotected	Average	Undrilled	Javelins	Light Spear	4	4–6	0–6	
Italian men-at-arms	Knights	Heavily Armoured	Average	Drilled	–	Lancers, Swordsmen	21	4	0–4	
Feudal men-at-arms	Only before 1466	Knights	Heavily Armoured	Superior	Undrilled	–	Lancers, Swordsmen	23	4	0–4
				Average				18		
Swiss pikemen and halberdiers	Only from 1480	Heavy Foot	Protected	Superior	Drilled	–	Pikemen	8	8–12	*8–16
Swiss crossbowmen		Light Foot	Unprotected	Average	Drilled	Crossbow		5	4	0–4
Swiss Handgunners		Light Foot	Unprotected	Average	Drilled	Firearm		4	4–6	0–8
Light guns	Light Artillery	–	Average	Undrilled	Light Artillery	–	15	2	0–2	
Heavy guns	Heavy Artillery	–	Average	Undrilled	Heavy Artillery	–	20	2	0–4	
Field fortifications or wagon laager	Field Fortifications						3	0–16		
Fortified camp							24	0–1		

FREE COMPANY

This list covers the Free Companies of unemployed soldiery arising during the various intervals of peace during the Hundred Years' War between 1357 and 1444 and operating in France, Spain and Italy. Individual companies usually numbered no more than a few hundred men, but army-sized conglomerations numbering over 10,000 were not uncommon, usually in the service of an employer, but occasionally, as in the case of the 16,000 strong Grand Company in the early 1360s, operating independently.

TROOP NOTES

We have assumed that conglomerations of mixed nationalities would initially retain national characteristics, but would tend to become homogenized and more disciplined (in battle, though very definitely not off the battlefield) if embodied for a longer period.

BUILDING A CUSTOMISED LIST USING OUR ARMY POINTS

Choose an army based on the maxima and minima in the list below. The following special instructions apply to this army:

Dismounted man-at-arms

FREE COMPANY

- Commanders should be depicted as men-at-arms.
- Mounted Gascon, French, Breton, Navarrese or Spanish men-at-arms (whether graded as Superior or Average when mounted) can always dismount as Superior, Heavily Armoured, Undrilled Heavy Foot – Heavy Weapon.
- Mounted mixed well-equipped Companions can always dismount as Average, Heavily Armoured, Drilled Heavy Foot – Heavy Weapon.
- Mounted less well-equipped Companions can always dismount as Average, Protected, Drilled Heavy Foot – Defensive Spearmen.

English Longbowman

FREE COMPANY

Territory Types: Agricultural, Woodlands

C-in-C		Inspired Commander/Field Commander/Troop Commander			80/50/35		1	
Sub-commanders		Field Commander			50		0–2	
		Troop Commander			35		0–3	

Troop name	Troop Type				Capabilities		Points per base	Bases per BG	Total bases
	Type	Armour	Quality	Training	Shooting	Close Combat			
Core Troops									
Dismounted men-at-arms and lesser Companions	Heavy Foot	Heavily Armoured	Superior	Undrilled	–	Heavy Weapon	14	4–8	10–32
	Heavy Foot	Heavily Armoured	Superior	Drilled	–	Heavy Weapon	16	4–8	
		Armoured	Superior				13		
		Armoured	Average				10		
English longbowmen	Medium Foot	Protected	Average	Drilled	Longbow	Swordsmen	9	6–8	0–24	10–48
Crossbowmen	Medium Foot	Protected	Average	Undrilled	Crossbow	–	6	6–8	0–16
				Drilled			7		
Gascon bidets or Bretons	Light Foot	Unprotected	Average	Undrilled	Javelins	Light Spear	4	4–6	0–6
Brigans or similar	Medium Foot	Protected	Average	Undrilled	–	Swordsmen	6	6–8	0–16
Ribauds or similar	Mob	Unprotected	Poor	Undrilled	–	–	2	6–8	0–8
Stakes to cover half the bases of each longbow BG	Only from 1415	Portable defences					3		All longbow BGs or none
Optional Troops									
Mounted Gascon, French, Breton, Navarrese or Spanish men-at-arms		Knights	Heavily Armoured	Superior	Undrilled	–	Lancers, Swordsmen	23	4–6	0–12
				Average				18		
Mounted mixed well-equipped Companions		Knights	Heavily Armoured	Average	Drilled	–	Lancers, Swordsmen	21	4–6	
Mounted less well-equipped Companions		Cavalry	Protected	Average	Drilled	–	Lancers, Swordsmen	10	4–6	
Bombards	Only in 1444	Heavy Artillery	–	Average	Undrilled	Heavy Artillery	–	20	2	0–2
Fortified camp								24		0–1

NAVARRESE

This list covers the armies of King Charles the Bad of Navarre during the Hundred Years' War, from his accession in 1350 until 1378 when the loss of his Norman possessions forced him to capitulate to the King of France. The forces of the Kingdom of Navarre itself were small compared with those of its neighbours. Charles supplemented his Navarrese forces with troops from his Norman possessions, and with English and Gascon mercenaries.

BUILDING A CUSTOMISED LIST USING OUR ARMY POINTS

Choose an army based on the maxima and minima in the list below. The following special instructions apply to this army:

- Commanders should be depicted as men-at-arms.
- Navarrese, Gascon or Norman men-at-arms (whether graded as Superior or Average when mounted) can always dismount as Superior, Heavily Armoured, Undrilled Heavy Foot – Heavy Weapon.
- The minimum marked * applies if any Gascon or English troops are used. Free Company ally commanders can only command Gascon and/or English troops. All Gascon and English troops must be under the command of a Free Company ally commander.

Navarrese foot soldier (crouched) in battle, mid-14th century, by Angus McBride. Taken from Men-at-Arms 200: El Cid and the Reconquista 1050–1492.

Free Company Allied Troop Commander.

NAVARRESE

Territory Types: Agricultural, Hilly, Mountains

C-in-C	Inspired Commander/Field Commander/Troop Commander						80/50/35		1
Sub-commanders	Field Commander/Troop Commander						50/35		0–2
Free Company allied commanders	Field Commander/Troop Commander						40/25		*1–2

Troop name	Troop Type				Capabilities		Points per base	Bases per BG	Total bases
	Type	Armour	Quality	Training	Shooting	Close Combat			
Core Troops									
Navarrese, Gascon, or Norman men-at-arms	Knights	Heavily Armoured	Superior	Undrilled	–	Lancers, Swordsmen	23	4–6	8–24
			Average				18		
Navarrese javelinmen	Medium Foot	Protected	Average	Undrilled	–	Light Spear	5	6–8	0–24
		Unprotected					4		
	Light Foot	Unprotected	Average	Undrilled	Javelins	Light Spear	4	6–8	
Navarrese slingers	Light Foot	Unprotected	Average	Undrilled	Sling	–	4	6–8	0–8
Optional Troops									
Gascon crossbowmen	Medium Foot	Protected	Average	Undrilled	Crossbow	–	6	6–8	0–12
Gascon bidets	Light Foot	Unprotected	Average	Undrilled	Javelins	Light Spear	4	6–8	0–8
Gascon brigans	Medium Foot	Protected	Average	Undrilled	–	Swordsmen	6	6–8	0–12
English men-at-arms	Heavy Foot	Heavily Armoured	Superior	Drilled	–	Heavy Weapon	16	4–6	0–6
English longbowmen	Medium Foot	Protected	Average	Drilled	Longbow	Swordsmen	9	6–8	0–12
Bombards	Heavy Artillery	–	Average	Undrilled	Heavy Artillery	–	20	2	0–2
Fortified camp							24		0–1

LATER LOW COUNTRIES

This list covers the armies of the Low Country communes from 1300 to 1477, and also the armies of Maximilian of Austria in the Low Countries from 1478 to 1500.

Low Countries communal armies could win frontal battles against mounted men-at-arms when terrain secured their flanks. They won thus against the French at Courtrai (1302). If, however, the enemy were able to threaten them from several directions, they could pin them in position. Like the Scots, they were then very vulnerable to archery. At Mons-en-Pevele (1304), the French were able to get the bulk of their forces behind the Lowland phalanx, but the Lowlanders had taken the precaution of protecting their rear with their baggage wagons, so the battle ended in a bloody draw. At Cassel (1328), an initial surprise attack by the Lowlanders on the French camps was repulsed with difficulty, thereafter the Lowlanders were surrounded and eventually routed. At Roosebeke (1382), the French mounted attack enveloped the Flemish flanks and broke the phalanx. At Othée (1408), the Burgundians surrounded the Liègeois phalanx and eventually routed it. At Rupelmonde (1452) the Gauntois were eventually broken by the archery of the Burgundian longbowmen.

Battle of Courtrai, 1302, by Angus McBride. Taken from Men-at-Arms 231: French Medieval Armies 1000–1300.

At Gavere (1453), a Burgundian archery barrage followed by a determined charge by mounted men-at-arms broke the Gauntois. At Brusthem (1467), the Liègeois were defeated by the Burgundian combination of dismounted men-at-arms and longbowmen.

After the defeat and death of Charles the Bold at Nancy in early 1477, the Low Countries rump of Charles's former territory resisted French attempts at annexation in the name of Charles's daughter Marie, who married Maximilian of Austria later that year. In 1478, new Ordonnance Companies were formed along the lines of those of Charles the Bold. In Maximilian's armies Swiss and German mercenaries replaced many of the Communal pikemen.

TROOP NOTES

Low country spearmen used very long spears but did not form up in especially deep formations at least until the mid-15th century. We therefore grade them as Offensive Spearmen rather than Pikemen. The plançon a picot was a long tapering club with an iron head and spike at the end. Several statutes were passed banning it, and it went out of favour at the end of the 14th century.

LATER LOW COUNTRIES STARTER ARMY		
Commander-in-Chief	1	Field Commander
Sub-commanders	2	2 x Troop Commander
Feudal men-at-arms	1 BG	4 bases of men-at-arms: Average, Heavily Armoured, Undrilled Knights – Lancers, Swordsmen
Spearmen	5 BGs	Each comprising 6 bases of spearmen: Average, Protected, Drilled Heavy Foot – Offensive Spearmen
Plançon wielders	1 BG	6 bases of plançon wielders: Average, Protected, Drilled Heavy Foot – Heavy Weapon
Crossbowmen	1 BG	8 bases of crossbowmen: Average, Protected, Drilled Medium Foot – Crossbow
Light guns	2 BGs	Each comprising 2 bases of light guns: Average, Undrilled Light Artillery – Light Artillery
Camp	1	Unfortified camp
Total	10 BGs	Camp, 4 mounted bases, 48 foot bases, 3 commanders

BUILDING A CUSTOMISED LIST USING OUR ARMY POINTS

Choose an army based on the maxima and minima in the list below. The following special instructions apply to this army:

- Commanders should be depicted as men-at-arms.
- Feudal men-at-arms (whether graded as Superior or Average when mounted) can always dismount as Superior, Heavily Armoured, Undrilled Heavy Foot – Heavy Weapon.

- Mercenary, Ordonnance or Burgher men-at-arms can always dismount as Average, Heavily Armoured, Drilled Heavy Foot – Heavy Weapon.
- The minimum marked * applies only before 1400.
- From 1478 a minimum of 4 Ordonnance men-at-arms must be included.

Mercenary man-at-arms

LATER LOW COUNTRIES

Territory Types: Agricultural, Developed

C-in-C	Inspired Commander/Field Commander/Troop Commander						80/50/35	1	
Sub-commanders	Field Commander						50	0–2	
	Troop Commander						35	0–3	

Troop name		Troop Type				Capabilities		Points per base	Bases per BG	Total bases
		Type	Armour	Quality	Training	Shooting	Close Combat			
Core Troops										
Feudal men-at-arms	Only before 1465	Knights	Heavily Armoured	Superior	Undrilled	–	Lancers, Swordsmen	23	4–6	
				Average				18		
	Any date	Knights	Heavily Armoured	Average	Undrilled	–	Swordsmen	17	4–6	0–12
Mercenary men-at-arms (or Ordonnance from 1478)		Knights	Heavily Armoured	Average	Drilled	–	Lancers, Swordsmen	21	4–6	
Burgher men-at-arms		Knights	Heavily Armoured	Average	Drilled	–	Swordsmen	20	4–6	
Spearmen	Only before 1450	Heavy Foot	Protected	Average	Drilled	–	Offensive Spearmen	8	6–10	24–112
Pikemen	Only from 1450	Heavy Foot	Protected	Average	Drilled	–	Pikemen	6	8–12	
Plançon wielders or Halberdiers		Heavy Foot	Protected	Average	Drilled	–	Heavy Weapon	8	4–8	*4–8
Crossbowmen		Medium Foot	Protected	Average	Drilled	Crossbow	–	7	4–8	4–8
Optional Troops										
Archers		Light Foot	Unprotected	Average	Drilled	Bow	–	5	4–6	0–6
		Medium Foot	Protected	Average	Drilled	Bow	–	7	4–6	
English longbowmen	1336 to 1477	Medium Foot	Protected	Average	Drilled	Longbow	Swordsmen	9	4–8	0–6
Ordonnance or English longbowmen	1478 to 1500									0–12
Stakes to cover half the bases of each longbow BG	Only from 1415	Portable defences						3		All longbow BGs or none
Swiss pikemen	Only from 1478 to 1479	Heavy Foot	Protected	Superior	Drilled	–	Pikemen	8	8	0–8
Handgunners	Only from 1410	Light Foot	Unprotected	Average	Drilled	Firearm	–	4	4–6	0–6
			Protected					5		
Light guns	Only from 1336	Light Artillery	–	Average	Undrilled	Light Artillery	–	15	2	0–6
Field defences or wagon laager		Field Fortifications						3		0–16
Fortified camp								24		0–1

LATER LOW COUNTRIES ALLIES

Allied commander		Field Commander/Troop Commander					40/25		1	
Troop name		Troop Type				Capabilities		Points per base	Bases per BG	Total bases
		Type	Armour	Quality	Training	Shooting	Close Combat			
Feudal men-at-arms	Only before 1465	Knights	Heavily Armoured	Superior	Undrilled	–	Lancers, Swordsmen	23	4	0–4
				Average				18		
	Any date	Knights	Heavily Armoured	Average	Undrilled	–	Swordsmen	17	4	
Mercenary men-at-arms (or Ordonnance from 1478)		Knights	Heavily Armoured	Average	Drilled	–	Lancers, Swordsmen	21	4	
Burgher men-at-arms		Knights	Heavily Armoured	Average	Drilled	–	Swordsmen	20	4	
Spearmen	Only before 1450	Heavy Foot	Protected	Average	Drilled	–	Offensive Spearmen	8	6–10	6–24
Pikemen	Only from 1450	Heavy Foot	Protected	Average	Drilled	–	Pikemen	6	8–12	
Plançon wielders or Halberdiers		Heavy Foot	Protected	Average	Drilled	–	Heavy Weapon	8	4	0–4
Crossbowmen		Medium Foot	Protected	Average	Drilled	Crossbow	–	7	4	0–4

MEDIEVAL BURGUNDIAN

This list covers Burgundian armies from 1363 until 1471, when Charles the Bold applied his Ordonnance reforms.

In 1363, Philip de Valois, fourth son of King John II of France, was granted the Duchy of Burgundy as Philip II (the Bold) thereof. In 1369, he married Margaret, Countess of Flanders, thus uniting these two rich territories. He later also acquired the County of Charolais. During the minority and subsequent insanity of his nephew Charles VI of France, he shared the regency with his brothers. In 1402, however, the King appointed his brother, Louis, Duke of Orléans, as regent instead. The latter's misrule resulted in Philip being appointed regent again in 1404, shortly before his death. His son John I (the Fearless) succeeded him. Almost immediately he came into conflict with Louis of Orléans. In 1407, on the orders of John the Fearless, Louis

was assassinated in Paris. He was attacked after mounting his horse by a party of men who rendered him defenceless by cutting off both his arms. In 1418, with the English holding much of northern France, John seized control of Paris from the Dauphin, the future Charles VII. In 1419, at a parley on the bridge at Montereau, John was assassinated by the Dauphin's followers. He was succeeded by his son, Philip III (the Good), who in 1420 allied himself with Henry V of England. The English alliance lasted until 1435. During his reign, Philip added many territories to his ancestral domain, including Namur, Hainault, Holland, Frisia, Brabant, Limburg, Antwerp and Luxembourg. He died in 1467, succeeded by his son Charles the Bold – who would attempt to consolidate his legacy into a kingdom, with ultimately fatal results for himself and his inheritance.

Siege of Vellexon, 1409–10, by Gerry Embleton. Taken from Men-at-Arms 144: Armies of Medieval Burgundy 1364–1477.

TROOP NOTES

The provision for feudal men-at-arms to lose their Lancers capability is based on Philippe de Commynes' eye-witness account of their performance at the battle of Montlhéry in 1465: "I do not believe that amongst the twelve hundred men-at-arms or thereabouts who were there fifty knew how to lay a lance in the arrêt.....because of the long peace."

Valet de guerre

MEDIEVAL BURGUNDIAN STARTER ARMY			
Commander-in-Chief	1	Field Commander	
Sub-commanders	2	2 x Troop Commander	
Feudal men-at-arms	2 BGs	Each comprising 6 bases of men-at-arms: Average, Heavily Armoured, Undrilled Knights – Lancers, Swordsmen	
English longbowmen	1 BG	8 bases of English longbowmen: Average, Protected, Drilled Medium Foot – Longbow, Swordsmen	
Picard longbowmen	1 BG	8 bases of Picard longbowmen: Average, Protected, Drilled Medium Foot – Longbow	
Feudal crossbowmen	1 BG	6 bases of crossbowmen: Average, Protected, Undrilled Medium Foot – Crossbow	
Low Countries spearmen	2 BGs	Each comprising 6 bases of spearmen: Poor, Protected, Drilled Heavy Foot – Offensive Spearmen	
Peasant levies	1 BG	8 bases of peasants: Poor, Unprotected, Undrilled Mob – no capabilities	
Camp	1	Unfortified camp	
Total	8 BGs	Camp, 12 mounted bases, 42 foot bases, 3 commanders	

BUILDING A CUSTOMISED LIST USING OUR ARMY POINTS

Choose an army based on the maxima and minima in the list below. The following special instructions apply to this army:

- Commanders should be depicted as men-at-arms.
- Burgundian or French men-at-arms (whether graded as Superior or Average when mounted) can always dismount as Superior, Heavily Armoured, Undrilled Heavy Foot – Heavy Weapon.
- Italian men-at-arms can always dismount as Average, Heavily Armoured, Drilled Heavy Foot – Heavy Weapon.
- The minimum marked * only applies before 1465.

- The minimum marked ** only applies from 1465.
- An English allied commander can only command English troops.

Charles the Bold

MEDIEVAL BURGUNDIAN

Territory Types: Agricultural, Developed

C-in-C	Inspired Commander/Field Commander/Troop Commander					80/50/35	1	
Sub-commanders	Field Commander					50	0–2	
	Troop Commander					35	0–3	

Troop name	Troop Type				Capabilities		Points per base	Bases per BG	Total bases
	Type	Armour	Quality	Training	Shooting	Close Combat			
Core Troops									
Burgundian or French men-at-arms	Knights	Heavily Armoured	Superior	Undrilled	–	Lancers, Swordsmen	23	4–6	*6–24
			Average				18		
Burgundian men-at-arms lacking skill with lance	Knights	Heavily Armoured	Average	Undrilled	–	Swordsmen	17	4–6	**6–18 / 8–24
Separately deployed valets de guerre	Cavalry	Armoured	Average	Undrilled	–	Lancers, Swordsmen	12	4–6	0–6
Feudal crossbowmen	Medium Foot	Protected	Average	Undrilled	Crossbow	–	6	6–8	6–16
Mercenary crossbowmen	Medium Foot	Protected	Average	Drilled	Crossbow	–	7	6–8	
Low countries crossbowmen	Medium Foot	Protected	Poor	Drilled	Crossbow	–	5	6–8	
Picard longbowmen	Medium Foot	Protected	Average	Drilled	Longbow	–	8	6–8	6–24
Stakes to cover half the bases of each longbow BG	Only from 1415	Portable defences					3		All longbow BGs or none
Optional Troops									
Italian men-at-arms	Knights	Heavily Armoured	Average	Drilled	–	Lancers, Swordsmen	21	4	0–4
English allied commander	Field Commander/Troop Commander						40/25	0–1	
English men-at-arms	Heavy Foot	Heavily Armoured	Superior	Drilled	–	Heavy Weapon	16	4	0–4
		Armoured	Superior				13		
		Armoured	Average				10		
English longbowmen	Medium Foot	Protected	Average	Drilled	Longbow	Swordsmen	9	6–8	0–8
Low Countries spearmen	Only before 1450	Heavy Foot	Protected	Poor	Drilled	–	Offensive Spearmen	6	6–10	0–16
Low Countries pikemen	Only from 1450	Heavy Foot	Protected	Poor	Drilled	–	Pikemen	4	8–12	0–16
Peasant levies	Mob	Unprotected	Poor	Undrilled	–	–	2	6–8	0–8
Handgunners	Only from 1430	Light Foot	Unprotected	Average	Drilled	Firearm	–	4	4	0–4
			Protected					5		
Swiss pikemen	Only from 1465	Heavy Foot	Protected	Superior	Drilled	–	Pikemen	8	4	0–4
Organ guns	Only from 1430	Light Artillery	–	Average	Undrilled	Light Artillery	–	15	2	0–4
Bombards	Heavy Artillery	–	Average	Undrilled	Heavy Artillery	–	20	2	0–2
Fortified camp							24		0–1

ORDONNANCE BURGUNDIAN

This list covers the armies of Duke Charles the Bold from 1471 when he first applied his Ordonnance reforms, until his final defeat and death in 1477.

CHARLES THE BOLD (1433 – 1477)

Duke of Burgundy from 1467 until his death in 1477, Charles the Bold appears to have had two main ambitions: To consolidate his scattered

territories into a Kingdom of Burgundy between France and Germany, and to have the best and most modern army in the world. He almost succeeded in both. He issued a series of ordinances resulting in the creation of a standing army intended to take the best of the tactical systems of western Europe and combine them into an unstoppable military machine. Drawing on Italian, English, French and German as well as Burgundian recruits, the intended army, as set out

Men-at-arms, 1471–77, by Gerry Embleton.
Taken from Men-at-Arms 144: Armies of Medieval Burgundy 1364–1477.

in the ordinance of 1472, comprised 3,600 men-at-arms (fully armoured "knights" and their more lightly armoured coustilliers and pages), 3,600 mounted longbowmen (who rode to battle but fought on foot), 1,200 foot longbowmen, 1,200 pikemen and 1,200 hand-gunners. The actual army raised was short by 600 mounted longbowmen and 600 hand-gunners, the shortfall being made up with crossbowmen and extra pikemen. Unfortunately, Charles' generalship did not match his organisational skills. In 1476 and 1477 he suffered a series of three disastrous defeats at the hands of the Swiss, who were allied with his enemy René, Duke of Lorraine. (See p.56). In the last of these, at Nancy, he was killed. His ambitions for a kingdom of Burgundy died with him. His possessions were divided between France and the Holy Roman Empire, and fought over for the next two centuries.

TROOP NOTES

The Ordonnance of 1473 specifies a mixed formation for pikemen and longbowmen. The pikemen were to advance in front of the archers so that the archers could fire over them as if over a wall. This formation was used by at least part of the foot at the battle of Grandson. A woodcut shows a unit of roughly equal numbers of archers and pike/voulge armed men behind a row of stakes. Accordingly, Ordonnance pikemen and longbowmen can be deployed in mixed battle groups of 6 bases, with a front rank of pikemen (counting as Defensive Spearmen) and rear rank of longbowmen. Philippe de Commynes in 1465 commented on the inability of the Burgundian feudal men-at-arms to use their lances properly. Low countries pikemen were unenthusiastic levies.

ORDONNANCE BURGUNDIAN STARTER ARMY		
Commander-in-Chief	1	Troop Commander (Charles the Bold)
Sub-commanders	2	2 x Troop Commander
Ordonnance men-at-arms	3 BGs	Each comprising 4 bases of men-at-arms: Average, Heavily Armoured, Drilled Knights – Lancers, Swordsmen
Ordonnance longbowmen	2 BGs	Each comprising 6 bases of longbowmen: Average, Protected, Drilled Medium Foot – Longbow, Swordsmen + Stakes (Portable Defences)
Ordonnance pikemen	1 BG	8 bases of pikemen: Average, Protected, Drilled Heavy Foot – Pikemen
Ordonnance handgunners	1 BG	6 bases of handgunners: Average, Unprotected, Drilled Light Foot – Firearm
Ordonnance crossbowmen	1 BG	4 bases of crossbowmen: Average, Protected, Drilled Medium Foot – Crossbow
Camp	1	Unfortified camp
Total	8 BGs	Camp, 12 mounted bases, 30 foot bases, 3 commanders

BUILDING A CUSTOMISED LIST USING OUR ARMY POINTS

Choose an army based on the maxima and minima in the list below. The following special instructions apply to this army:

- Commanders should be depicted as men-at-arms.
- Ordonnance or other mercenary men-at-arms can always dismount as Average, Heavily Armoured, Drilled Heavy Foot – Heavy Weapon.

- Household gendarmes can always dismount as Superior, Heavily Armoured, Drilled Heavy Foot – Heavy Weapon.

- Feudal men-at-arms can always dismount as Superior, Heavily Armoured, Undrilled Heavy Foot – Heavy Weapon.

ORDONNANCE BURGUNDIAN

Territory Types: Agricultural, Developed

Troop name	Troop Type				Capabilities		Points per base	Bases per BG	Total bases
	Type	Armour	Quality	Training	Shooting	Close Combat			
C-in-C	Field Commander/Troop Commander						50/35	1	
Sub-commanders	Field Commander						50	0–2	
	Troop Commander						35	0–3	
Core Troops									
Ordonnance or other mercenary men-at-arms	Knights	Heavily Armoured	Average	Drilled	–	Lancers, Swordsmen	21	4–6	8–24
Ordonnance longbowmen	Medium Foot	Protected	Average	Drilled	Longbow	Swordsmen	9	6–8	6–20
Ordonnance pikemen and vougliers	Heavy Foot	Protected	Average	Drilled	–	Pikemen	6	8	0–9
Mixed BGs each replacing 3 pikemen and 3 longbowmen	Heavy Foot	Protected	Average	Drilled	–	Defensive Spearmen	7	1/2	6	0–18
	Medium Foot	Protected	Average	Drilled	Longbow	Swordsmen	9	1/2	
Stakes to cover half the bases of each longbow and mixed BG	Portable defences						3		All such BGs or none
Ordonnance crossbowmen	Medium Foot	Protected	Average	Drilled	Crossbow	–	7	4	0–4
Ordonnance handgunners	Light Foot	Unprotected	Average	Drilled	Firearm	–	4	4–6	0–6
		Protected					5		
Optional Troops									
Household gendarmes	Knights	Heavily Armoured	Superior	Drilled	–	Lancers, Swordsmen	26	2	0–2
Italian mounted crossbowmen	Light Horse	Unprotected	Average	Drilled	Crossbow	–	7	4	0–4
Italian foot crossbowmen	Medium Foot	Protected	Average	Drilled	Crossbow	–	7	4–6	0–6
Feudal men-at-arms	Knights	Heavily Armoured	Average	Undrilled	–	Swordsmen	17	4	0–4
Feudal crossbowmen	Medium Foot	Protected	Average	Undrilled	Crossbow	–	6	4	0–4
Low Countries pikemen	Heavy Foot	Protected	Poor	Drilled	–	Pikemen	4	8–12	0–12
Light guns	Light Artillery	–	Average	Undrilled	Light Artillery	–	15	2	0–6
Heavy guns	Heavy Artillery	–	Average	Undrilled	Heavy Artillery	–	20	2	0–4
Field fortifications	Field Fortifications						3		0–16
Fortified camp							24		0–1
Allies									
Yorkist English allies – Wars of the Roses English									

SWISS

This list covers Swiss armies from 1291, when the Forest Cantons – Uri, Schwyz and Unterwalten – formed the Everlasting League, until 1500.

The Swiss fought in deep infantry columns. For the first hundred years of the period, they relied on their murderous halberds and their native terrain. At Mortgarten (1315), they ambushed the Austrians while they were in column of march along a lake-side path. The Austrians were massacred. At Laupen (1339), the Swiss adopted a defensive position on a hill. The Burgundians and allies attacked this position. The allied foot were easily defeated by the Bernese and other Swiss facing them. The mounted allied men-at-arms were initially successful against the Forest Canton troops facing them, but were ultimately defeated when the victorious Bernese contingent joined the fight against them. At Sempach (1386), the armies met while in column of march. The Austrians dismounted their men-at-arms and advanced in column on foot against the Swiss vanguard, the Lucerne contingent. The battle was going badly for the Swiss when the rest of their force, mainly from Uri, arrived. The battle then swung in favour of the Swiss and the Austrians eventually fled. Vögelinsegg (1403) and Stoss (1405) were successful ambushes against Austrian forces.

Around the turn of the century, the Swiss began to replace their halberds with pikes, which appear to have been more effective against both mounted and dismounted men-at-arms in open ground. By the time of Arbedo (1422), about a third were armed with pikes, the remainder still having halberds. Initial mounted attacks by the Milanese men-at-arms were repulsed with heavy losses. Carmagnola, the Milanese commander,

then ordered his men-at-arms to dismount. A severe struggle ensued, in which the Swiss came off worse. The timely arrival of 600 Swiss foragers, however, was mistaken for major reinforcements by the enemy. They pulled back, allowing the Swiss to retire from the field in good order.

By the mid-15th century, the Swiss had largely switched to pikes, attacking rapidly in huge columns. Each such column had a core of halberdiers who could sally out to cause mayhem if the column was halted. There were usually three such columns, the Vorhut (vanguard), Gewalthut (centre) and Nachhut (rearguard), attacking in echelon. The Vorhut usually included most of the army's crossbowmen and handgunners.

At Grandson (1476), against Charles the Bold of Burgundy, the action started accidentally between the Swiss Vorhut and the Burgundian vanguard. Several attacks by mounted men-at-arms were repulsed by the Swiss. Thinking that the Vorhut was the whole Swiss army, Charles then started to redeploy his army in an attempt to draw the Swiss into a pocket with archers and artillery shooting into each flank. Unfortunately, while this redeployment was in progress, the Swiss Gewalthut and Nachhut arrived. The Burgundian troops, misinterpreting the redeployment as a retreat, panicked and fled. At Morat (1476), Charles deployed his forces behind a ditch and palisade in expectation of a Swiss attack. On the morning of the battle, however, not realising that the Swiss were close, he stood down most of his forces. When the Swiss arrived, the forces remaining under arms proved inadequate to stop them and the rest of the Burgundian forces, coming up piecemeal, were easily defeated. At Nancy (1477), Charles adopted a strong defensive position with his foot

Swiss footsoldiers, by Gerry Embleton. Taken from Men-at-Arms 94: The Swiss at War 1300–1500.

and dismounted men-at-arms in the centre, and mounted men-at-arms on each wing. Rather than attack this formidable array frontally, the Swiss sent their Vorhut to attack the Burgundian left from the front, and their larger Gewalthut to hook round through wooded hills and attack the Burgundian right from the flank. The Nachhut, consisting only of handgunners, screened the gap between the two main Swiss bodies. Decisively outmanoeuvred, the

Halberdiers of the Burgundian Wars, by Gerry Embleton.
Taken from Men-at-Arms 94: The Swiss at War 1300–1500.

Burgundians were defeated again, and Charles himself was killed in the rout.

From the early 15th century, the Swiss hired themselves out en bloc to neighbouring states as mercenaries. The first example of this was in 1424, when Florence hired the services of 10,000 Swiss for 3 months. From 1480, the Kings of France hired Swiss mercenaries on a regular basis, numbering around 6,000 in the reign of Louis XI.

TROOP NOTES

Halberdiers in the centre of pike blocks are treated as pikemen. We rather generously allow the stones thrown by the "enfants perdus" at Laupen to be treated as javelins. Letzinen were stone barricades used to block roads so that the enemy could be halted and ambushed.

Halberdier

SWISS STARTER ARMY		
Commander-in-Chief	1	Field Commander
Sub-commanders	2	1 Field Commander, 1 x Troop Commander
Pikemen	5 BGs	Each comprising 8 bases of pikemen: Superior, Protected, Drilled Heavy Foot – Pikemen
Handgunners	3 BGs	Each comprising 6 bases of handgunners: Average, Unprotected, Drilled Light Foot – Firearm
Crossbowmen	1 BG	8 bases of crossbowmen: Average, Unprotected, Drilled Light Foot – Crossbow
Mounted crossbowmen	1 BG	4 bases of mounted crossbowmen: Average, Unprotected, Drilled Light Horse - Crossbow
Camp	1	Unfortified camp
Total	10 BGs	Camp, 4 mounted bases, 66 foot bases, 3 commanders

BUILDING A CUSTOMISED LIST USING OUR ARMY POINTS

Choose an army based on the maxima and minima in the list below. The following special instructions apply to this army:

• Commanders should be depicted as halberdiers or pikemen.

Swiss Infantry

SWISS

Territory Types: Mountains

C-in-C	Inspired Commander/Field Commander/Troop Commander						80/50/35	1	
Sub-commanders	Field Commander						50	0–2	
	Troop Commander						35	0–3	

Troop name	Troop Type				Capabilities		Points per base	Bases per BG	Total bases
	Type	Armour	Quality	Training	Shooting	Close Combat			
Core Troops									
Halberdiers	Before 1425	Heavy Foot	Protected	Superior	Drilled	–	Heavy Weapon	10	8–12	16–96
	1425 to 1490								4–8	0–24
Pikemen	1360 to 1421	Heavy Foot	Protected	Superior	Drilled	–	Pikemen	8	8–12	8–32
	From 1422									24–120
Crossbowmen	Before 1476	Light Foot	Unprotected	Average	Drilled	Crossbow	–	5	4–8	4–20
	From 1476									0–8
Handgunners	1400 to 1475	Light Foot	Unprotected	Average	Drilled	Firearm	–	4	4–8	0–8
	From 1476									4–20
Optional Troops									
Mounted crossbowmen		Light Horse	Unprotected	Average	Drilled	Crossbow	–	7	4	0–4
"Enfant perdus" throwing stones	Only before 1360	Light Foot	Unprotected	Poor	Undrilled	Javelins	–	2	6–8	0–8
Light guns	Only from 1360	Light Artillery	–	Average	Undrilled	Light Artillery	–	15	2	0–2
Letzinen – stone barricades	Only before 1422	Field Fortifications						3		0–12
Fortified camp								24		0–1
Special Campaigns									
The Burgundian War 1476 to 1477										
René, Duc de Lorraine (sub-commander)	Field Commander/Troop Commander						50/35	1	
Knights and men-at-arms		Knights	Average	Drilled	Heavily Armoured	–	Lancers, Swordsmen	21	4–8	4–8

SWISS ALLIES

Allied commander	Field Commander/Troop Commander						40/25	1	

Troop name	Troop Type				Capabilities		Points per base	Bases per BG	Total bases
	Type	Armour	Quality	Training	Shooting	Close Combat			
Halberdiers	Before 1425	Heavy Foot	Protected	Superior	Drilled	–	Heavy Weapon	10	8–12	8–24
	1425 to 1490								4–8	0–8
Pikemen	1360 to 1421	Heavy Foot	Protected	Superior	Drilled	–	Pikemen	8	8–12	0–8
	From 1422									8–24
Crossbowmen	Before 1476	Light Foot	Unprotected	Average	Drilled	Crossbow	–	5	4–6	4–6
	From 1476									0–4
Handgunners	Before 1476	Light Foot	Unprotected	Average	Drilled	Firearm	–	4	4–6	0–4
	From 1476									4–6

LATER MEDIEVAL GERMAN

This list covers armies of the Holy Roman Empire from 1340 to 1500, apart from those fringes covered by their own army lists.

LATER MEDIEVAL GERMAN STARTER ARMY		
Commander-in-Chief	1	Field Commander
Sub-commanders	2	2 x Troop Commander
Feudal men-at-arms	2 BGs	Each comprising 4 bases of men-at-arms: Superior, Heavily Armoured, Undrilled Knights – Lancers, Swordsmen
Mounted crossbowmen	1 BG	4 bases of mounted crossbowmen: Average, Armoured, Drilled Cavalry – Crossbow, Swordsmen
Halberdiers	1 BG	6 bases of halberdiers: Average, Armoured, Drilled Heavy Foot – Heavy Weapon
Spearmen	2 BGs	Each comprising 6 bases of spearmen: Average, Protected, Drilled Heavy Foot – Defensive Spearmen
Crossbowmen	2 BGs	Each comprising 6 bases of crossbowmen: Average, Protected, Drilled Medium Foot – Crossbow
Camp	1	Unfortified camp
Total	8 BGs	Camp, 12 mounted bases, 30 foot bases, 3 commanders

BUILDING A CUSTOMISED LIST USING OUR ARMY POINTS

Choose an army based on the maxima and minima in the list below. The following special instructions apply to this army:

- Commanders should be depicted as men-at-arms.
- Feudal men-at-arms can always dismount as Superior, Heavily Armoured, Undrilled Heavy Foot – Heavy Weapon.
- Mercenary men-at-arms can always dismount as Average, Heavily Armoured, Drilled Heavy Foot – Heavy Weapon.
- Hungarians cannot be used with Swiss.

Mercenary man-at-arms

LATER MEDIEVAL GERMAN

Territory Types: Agricultural, Developed, Hilly

C-in-C		Inspired Commander/Field Commander/Troop Commander					80/50/35		1	
Sub-commanders		Field Commander					50		0-2	
		Troop Commander					35		0-3	
Troop name		**Troop Type**			**Capabilities**		**Points per base**	**Bases per BG**	**Total bases**	
		Type	Armour	Quality	Training	Shooting	Impact			

Troop name		Type	Armour	Quality	Training	Shooting	Impact	Points per base	Bases per BG	Total bases	
Core Troops											
Feudal men-at-arms	Only before 1450	Knights	Heavily Armoured	Superior	Undrilled	–	Lancers, Swordsmen	23	4-6	6-24	6-24
Mercenary men-at-arms		Knights	Heavily Armoured	Average	Drilled	–	Lancers, Swordsmen	21	4-6		
Lighter men-at-arms	Only from 1450	Cavalry	Armoured	Average	Drilled	–	Lancers, Swordsmen	13	4-6	0-8	
Mounted Crossbowmen		Cavalry	Armoured	Average	Drilled	Crossbow	Swordsmen	14	4-6	0-8	0-8
Mounted handgunners	Only from 1450	Cavalry	Armoured	Average	Drilled	Firearm	Swordsmen	13	4	0-4	
Spearmen	Only before 1450	Heavy Foot	Protected	Average	Drilled	–	Defensive Spearmen	7	6-8	0-24	8-24
			Protected	Poor				5			
		Heavy Foot	Armoured	Average	Drilled	–	Defensive Spearmen	9		0-12	
			Armoured	Poor				7			
Low Countries spearmen	Only before 1450	Heavy Foot	Protected	Average	Drilled	–	Offensive Spearmen	8	6-10	0-12	
				Poor				6			
Halberdiers or axemen		Heavy Foot	Protected	Average	Drilled	–	Heavy Weapon	8	4-8	0-8	
			Armoured					10			
Pikemen	Only from 1450	Heavy Foot	Protected	Average	Drilled	–	Pikemen	6	8-12	12-32	
				Poor				4			
Crossbowmen		Medium Foot	Protected	Average	Drilled	Crossbow	–	7	6-8	6-24	6-24
				Poor				5			
		Light Foot	Unprotected	Average	Drilled	Crossbow	–	5	6-8		
				Poor				3			
Archers		Medium Foot	Protected	Average	Drilled	Bow	–	7	6-8	0-8	
				Poor				5			
		Light Foot	Unprotected	Average	Drilled	Bow	–	5	6-8		
				Poor				3			
Handgunners	Only from 1375	Light Foot	Unprotected	Average	Drilled	Firearm	–	4	4-8	0-8	
			Protected					5			
Optional Troops											
Heerban		Mob	Unprotected	Poor	Undrilled	–	–	2	8-12	0-12	
Free Canton spearmen		Medium Foot	Unprotected	Average	Undrilled	–	Offensive Spearmen	6	6-8	0-24	
			Protected					7			
War wagons	Only from 1425	Battle Wagons	–	Average	Undrilled	Crossbow	Heavy Weapon	23	2-4	0-8	
Light guns	Any date	Light Artillery	–	Average	Undrilled	Light Artillery	–	15	2	0-2	
	Only from 1425	Battle Wagons	–	Average	Undrilled	Light Artillery	–	20	2		
Heavy guns	Only from 1375	Heavy Artillery	–	Average	Undrilled	Heavy Artillery	–	20	2	0-2	
Fortified camp								24		0-1	

LATER MEDIEVAL GERMAN

Allies									
Swiss allies									
Special Campaigns									
Only Imperial armies from 1420 to 1457									
Hungarians	Light Horse	Unprotected	Average	Undrilled	Bow	–	8	4–6	0–8

German Medieval Knights, by Angus McBride.
Taken from *Men-at-Arms 166: German Medieval Armies 1300–1500.*

LATER MEDIEVAL GERMAN ALLIES

Allied commander		\multicolumn{6}{c}{Field Commander/Troop Commander}				40/25		1	
Troop name		\multicolumn{5}{c}{Troop Type}			\multicolumn{2}{c}{Capabilities}	Points per base	Bases per BG	\multicolumn{2}{c}{Total bases}
		Type	Armour	Quality	Training	Shooting	Impact				
Feudal men-at-arms	Only before 1450	Knights	Heavily Armoured	Superior	Undrilled	–	Lancers, Swordsmen	23	4–6	4–8	
Mercenary men-at-arms		Knights	Heavily Armoured	Average	Drilled	–	Lancers, Swordsmen	21	4–6		
Lighter men-at-arms	Only from 1450	Cavalry	Armoured	Average	Drilled	–	Lancers, Swordsmen	13	4	0–4	
Mounted Crossbowmen		Cavalry	Armoured	Average	Drilled	Crossbow	Swordsmen	14	4		
Spearmen	Only before 1450	Heavy Foot	Protected	Average	Drilled	–	Defensive Spearmen	7	6–8	0–12	6–12
			Protected	Poor		–	Defensive Spearmen	5			
		Heavy Foot	Armoured	Average	Drilled	–	Defensive Spearmen	9		0–6	
			Armoured	Poor		–	Defensive Spearmen	7			
Halberdiers or axemen		Heavy Foot	Protected	Average	Drilled	–	Heavy Weapon	8	4	0–4	
			Armoured			–		10			
Pikemen	Only from 1450	Heavy Foot	Protected	Average	Drilled	–	Pikemen	6	8–12	8–12	
				Poor		–		4			
Crossbowmen		Medium Foot	Protected	Average	Drilled	Crossbow	–	7	4–8	4–8	
				Poor			–	5			
Handgunners	Only from 1375	Light Foot	Unprotected	Average	Drilled	Firearm	–	4	4	0–4	
			Protected				–	5			

LATER MEDIEVAL DANISH

This list covers the armies of the Kingdom of Denmark from 1300 until the Union of Kalmar in 1397 when Denmark, Norway and Sweden were officially united under one crown, and then Union armies until 1500.

German Mercenary Halberdier

TROOP NOTES

Danish and Union armies made much use of German mercenaries. Scandinavian armour styles were somewhat old-fashioned in the 14th century, but caught up with more modern European styles in the 15th. The select levy were armed with halberds or other pole-arms. The general levy were mostly armed with short spears.

LATER MEDIEVAL DANISH STARTER ARMY

Commander-in-Chief	1	Field Commander
Sub-commanders	2	2 x Troop Commander
Feudal men-at-arms	2 BG	Each comprising 4 bases of men-at-arms: Superior, Heavily Armoured, Undrilled Knights – Lancers, Swordsmen
Mounted crossbowmen	1 BG	4 bases of mounted crossbowmen: Average, Armoured, Undrilled Cavalry – Crossbow, Swordsmen
Select levy	2 BGs	Each comprising 6 bases of select levy: Half Average, Armoured, Drilled Heavy Foot – Heavy Weapon, half Average, Armoured, Drilled Medium Foot – Crossbow, Swordsmen
German mercenary pikemen	2 BGs	Each comprising 8 bases of pikemen: Average, Protected, Drilled Heavy Foot – Pikemen
Handgunners	1 BG	6 bases of handgunners: Average, Unprotected, Drilled Light Foot – Firearm
Camp	1	Unfortified camp
Total	8 BGs	Camp, 12 mounted bases, 32 foot bases, 3 commanders

The battle of Brunkenberg, 1471, by Angus McBride.
Taken from Men-at-Arms 399: Medieval Scandinavian Armies (2) 1300–1500.

BUILDING A CUSTOMISED LIST USING OUR ARMY POINTS

Choose an army based on the maxima and minima in the list below. The following special instructions apply to this army:

- Commanders should be depicted as men-at-arms.

LATER MEDIEVAL DANISH										
Territory Types: Agricultural, Woodland										
C-in-C	Inspired Commander/Field Commander/Troop Commander						80/50/35	1		
Sub-commanders	Field Commander						50	0–2		
	Troop Commander						35	0–3		
Troop name	Troop Type				Capabilities		Points per base	Bases per BG	Total bases	
	Type	Armour	Quality	Training	Shooting	Close Combat				
Core Troops										
Feudal men-at-arms	Knights	Heavily Armoured	Superior	Undrilled	–	Lancers, Swordsmen	23	4–6	4–16	
			Average				18			
Select levy	Heavy Foot	Armoured	Average	Drilled	–	Heavy Weapon	10	1/2 or all	6–8	12–24
				Undrilled			9			
	Medium Foot	Armoured	Average	Drilled	Crossbow	Swordsmen	10	1/2 or none		
				Undrilled			9			
General levy	Heavy Foot	Protected	Poor	Undrilled	–	Defensive spearmen	4	1/2, 2/3 or all	6–9	0–36
	Light Foot	Unprotected	Poor	Undrilled	Crossbow	–	3	1/2, 1/3 or none		
					Bow		3			
Optional Troops										
Separately deployed mounted attendants	Cavalry	Protected	Average	Undrilled	–	Swordsmen	8	4	0–4	
			Poor				6			
Mounted crossbowmen	Cavalry	Armoured	Average	Undrilled	Crossbow	Swordsmen	13	4–6	0–8	0–8
Mounted handgunners	Only from 1450	Cavalry	Armoured	Average	Undrilled	Firearm	Swordsmen	12	4	0–4
German mercenary men-at-arms	Knights	Heavily Armoured	Average	Drilled	–	Lancers, Swordsmen	21	4–6	0–8	
German mercenary halberdiers	Only before 1488	Heavy Foot	Armoured	Average	Drilled	–	Heavy Weapon	10	4–6	0–6
German mercenary pikemen and halberdiers	Only from 1488	Heavy Foot	Protected	Average	Drilled	–	Pikemen	6	8–12	0–16
Handgunners	Only from 1397	Light Foot	Unprotected	Average	Drilled	Firearm	–	4	4–6	0–6
			Protected					5		
Light guns	Only from 1397	Light Artillery	–	Average	Undrilled	Light Artillery	–	15	2	0–4	0–4
Bombards	Only from 1397	Heavy Artillery	–	Average	Undrilled	Heavy Artillery	–	20	2	0–2	
Fortified camp							24	0–1		
Allies										
German allies – Later Medieval German										
Swedish allies (Only from 1397) – Later Medieval Swedish										

LATER MEDIEVAL SWEDISH

This list covers the armies of the Kingdom of Sweden from 1300 until the Union of Kalmar in 1397 when Denmark, Norway and Sweden were officially united under one crown, and then anti-Union Swedish armies until 1500.

TROOP NOTES

Swedish peasant militia were particularly well armoured and effective, fighting in mixed units of men with crossbow or longbow and men with pole-arms, axes, spears etc. The proportion of pole-arms increased as time went on. The crossbow was far more common than the longbow. As it seems unlikely that crossbows and longbows were deployed in separate units, the mixture is treated as crossbows. Scandinavian armour styles were somewhat old-fashioned in the 14th century, but caught up with more modern European styles in the 15th. Ambushes were popular, timber barricades being used to block routes through woodland.

Mounted Crossbowman

Swedish troops vs Danish man-at-arms, by Angus McBride. Taken from Men-at-Arms 399: Medieval Scandinavian Armies (2) 1300–1500.

LATER MEDIEVAL SWEDISH STARTER ARMY		
Commander-in-Chief	1	Field Commander
Sub-commanders	2	2 x Troop Commander
Feudal men-at-arms	1 BG	4 bases of men-at-arms: Superior, Heavily Armoured, Undrilled Knights – Lancers, Swordsmen
Mounted crossbowmen	1 BG	4 bases of mounted crossbowmen: Average, Armoured, Undrilled Cavalry – Crossbow, Swordsmen
Militia	6 BGs	Each comprising 6 bases of militia: Half Average, Armoured, Undrilled Heavy Foot – Heavy Weapon, half Average, Armoured, Undrilled Medium Foot – Crossbow, Swordsmen
Camp	1	Unfortified camp
Total	8 BGs	Camp, 8 mounted bases, 36 foot bases, 3 commanders

BUILDING A CUSTOMISED LIST USING OUR ARMY POINTS

Choose an army based on the maxima and minima in the list below. The following special instructions apply to this army:

- Commanders should be depicted as men-at-arms.

LATER MEDIEVAL SWEDISH									
Territory Types: Agricultural, Woodland									
C-in-C	Inspired Commander/Field Commander/Troop Commander						80/50/35	1	
Sub-commanders	Field Commander						50	0–2	
	Troop Commander						35	0–3	
Troop name	Troop Type				Capabilities		Points per base	Bases per BG	Total bases
	Type	Armour	Quality	Training	Shooting	Impact			
Core Troops									
Feudal men-at-arms	Knights	Heavily Armoured	Superior	Undrilled	–	Lancers, Swordsmen	23	4–6	4–12
			Average				18		
Militia	Heavy Foot	Armoured	Average	Undrilled	–	Heavy Weapon	9	1/2	18–80
								6–8	
	Medium Foot	Armoured	Average	Undrilled	Crossbow	Swordsmen	9	1/2	
Optional Troops									
Separately deployed mounted attendants	Cavalry	Protected	Average	Undrilled	–	Swordsmen	8	4	0–4
			Poor				6		
Mounted crossbowmen	Cavalry	Armoured	Average	Undrilled	Crossbow	Swordsmen	13	4–6	0–8	0–8
Mounted handgunners	Only from 1450	Cavalry	Armoured	Average	Undrilled	Firearm	Swordsmen	12	4	0–4
Handgunners	Only from 1397	Light Foot	Protected	Average	Drilled	Firearm	–	5	4–6	0–6
Light guns	Only from 1397	Light Artillery	–	Average	Undrilled	Light Artillery	–	15	2	0–4	0–4
Bombards	Only from 1397	Heavy Artillery	–	Average	Undrilled	Heavy Artillery	–	20	2	0–2
Barricades	Field Fortifications						3		0–24
Fortified camp							24		0–1

LATER MEDIEVAL SWEDISH ALLIES

Allied commander	Field Commander/Troop Commander						40/25		1	
Troop name	Troop Type				Capabilities		Points per base	Bases per BG	Total bases	
	Type	Armour	Quality	Training	Shooting	Impact				
Feudal men-at-arms	Knights	Heavily Armoured	Superior	Undrilled	–	Lancers, Swordsmen	23	4	0–4	
			Average				18			
Militia	Heavy Foot	Armoured	Average	Undrilled	–	Heavy Weapon	9	1/2	6–8	6–24
	Medium Foot	Armoured	Average	Undrilled	Crossbow	Swordsmen	9	1/2		

CONDOTTA ITALIAN

This list covers Italian armies from 1320 to 1500. It differs from other lists in having special sections to represent the additional options available to the major Italian states.

TROOP NOTES

Most men-at-arms were raised by contracts (condotte) with mercenary captains, though some (lanze spezzati) were hired individually by the state. Traditional communal militia infantry were neither enthusiastic nor highly regarded, and only Florence's out-of-date army made much use of them in the later part of the period. By then, most infantry were provisionati, paid soldiers hired directly by the state, though some were raised by condotte. Militia pavisier and crossbowmen battle groups represent several ranks of crossbowmen with a rank of spear-armed pavisiers in front. They are best depicted as front rank bases of pavisier figures and rear rank bases of crossbowmen figures.

MILANESE STARTER ARMY

Commander-in-Chief	1	Field Commander
Sub-commanders	2	2 x Troop Commander
Mercenary men-at-arms	2 BGs	Each comprising 6 bases of men-at-arms: Average, Heavily Armoured, Drilled Knights – Lancers, Swordsmen
Mounted crossbowmen	1 BG	6 bases of mounted crossbowmen: Average, Unprotected, Drilled Light Horse – Crossbow
Pikemen	1 BGs	12 bases of pikemen: Average, Protected, Drilled Heavy Foot – Pikemen
Billmen	2 BGs	Each comprising 4 bases of billmen: Average, Protected, Drilled Heavy Foot – Heavy Weapon
Handgunners	2 BGs	Each comprising 6 bases of handgunners: Average, Unprotected, Drilled Light Foot – Firearm
Camp	1	Unfortified camp
Total	8 BGs	Camp, 18 mounted bases, 32 foot bases, 3 commanders

BUILDING A CUSTOMISED LIST USING OUR ARMY POINTS

Choose an army based on the maxima and minima in the list below. The following special instructions apply to this army:

- Commanders should be depicted as men-at-arms.
- Except for Florentine armies, at least one third of the army's bases (not including commanders or allies) must be mounted troops.
- Venetians outside Italy cannot use spearmen or pikemen.
- Italian allies can be from any of the main states. Troops are taken from the main list and count towards main list minima and maxima. Special options (not allies) belonging to the allied state can be used (except options for Venice outside Italy), but only one minimum-sized battle group of each.
- Mercenary men-at-arms can always dismount as Average, Heavily Armoured, Drilled Heavy Foot – Heavy Weapon.
- Famiglia ducale can always dismount as Superior, Heavily Armoured, Drilled Heavy Foot – Heavy Weapon.
- Feudal or Dalmatian men-at-arms can always dismount as Superior, Heavily Armoured, Undrilled Heavy Foot – Heavy Weapon.

Papal Guardsman and Sword and Buckler man

Condottiere column on the march, late 14th century, by Graham Turner. Taken from Warrior 115: Condottiere 1300–1500.

CONDOTTA ITALIAN

Territory Types: Agricultural, Developed, Hilly									
C-in-C	Inspired Commander/Field Commander/Troop Commander						80/50/35	1	
Sub-commanders	Field Commander						50	0–2	
	Troop Commander						35	0–3	
Troop name	Troop Type				Capabilities		Points per base	Bases per BG	Total bases
	Type	Armour	Quality	Training	Shooting	Close Combat			
Core Troops									
Mercenary men-at-arms	Knights	Heavily Armoured	Average	Drilled	–	Lancers, Swordsmen	21	4–6	10–36
Optional Troops									
Mounted crossbowmen	Light Horse	Unprotected	Average	Drilled	Crossbow	–	7	4–6	0–8
Crossbowmen	Medium Foot	Protected	Average	Drilled	Crossbow	–	7	4–8	0–12
	Light Foot	Unprotected	Average	Drilled	Crossbow	–	5	4–8	
Pikemen	Only from 1400	Heavy Foot	Protected	Average	Drilled	–	Pikemen	6	8–12	0–12
Billmen or halberdiers	Only from 1400	Heavy Foot	Protected	Average	Drilled	–	Heavy Weapon	8	4–6	0–8
Javelinmen		Medium Foot	Protected	Average	Drilled	–	Light Spear	6	4–6	
Swordsmen		Medium Foot	Protected	Average	Drilled	–	Swordsmen	7	4–6	
Sword and buckler men	Only from 1416	Medium Foot	Protected	Average	Drilled	–	Skilled Swordsmen	8	4–6	
Handgunners	1400 to 1439	Light Foot	Unprotected	Average	Drilled	Firearm	–	4	4	0–4
			Protected					5		
	From 1440	Light Foot	Unprotected	Average	Drilled	Firearm	–	4	4–6	0–12
			Protected					5		
Militia spearmen	Only before 1400 or Florence at any date	Heavy Foot	Protected	Poor	Drilled	–	Defensive Spearmen	5	6–8	0–8
Militia pavisiers and crossbowmen	Only before 1400 or Florence at any date	Heavy Foot	Protected	Poor	Drilled	–	Defensive Spearmen	5	1/2	6	0–12
		Medium Foot	Protected	Poor	Drilled	Crossbow	–	5	1/2	
Militia crossbowmen		Light Foot	Unprotected	Poor	Drilled	Crossbow	–	3	6–8	
Organ guns		Light Artillery	–	Average	Undrilled	Light Artillery	–	15	2	0–2
Bombards		Heavy Artillery	–	Average	Undrilled	Heavy Artillery	–	20	2	0–2
Field fortifications		Field Fortifications						3		0–12
Fortified camp								24		0–1
Allies										
Italian allies – up to 2 contingents – see notes above										
Florence										
Hungarians	Only before 1440	Light Horse	Unprotected	Average	Undrilled	Bow	–	8	4–6	0–6
English archers	Only before 1400	Medium Foot	Protected	Average	Drilled	Longbow	Swordsmen	9	4–8	0–8
	Only from 1400 to 1440									0–4
Stakes to cover half the bases of longbow BG	Only from 1415	Portable defences						3		All or none

Upgrade militia spearmen to pikemen	Only from 1400	Heavy Foot	Protected	Poor	Drilled	–	Pikemen	4	8	0–8
Swiss mercenary allies (Only in 1424)										
Milan										
Famiglia ducale		Knights	Heavily Armoured	Superior	Drilled	–	Lancers, Swordsmen	26	2–4	0–4
Naples										
Guardsmen		Heavy Foot	Protected	Superior	Drilled	–	Defensive Spearmen	9	4	0–4
Feudal men-at-arms		Knights	Heavily Armoured	Superior	Undrilled	–	Lancers, Swordsmen	23	4–6	0–8
Hungarians	Only before 1440	Light Horse	Unprotected	Average	Undrilled	Bow	–	8	4–6	0–6
Aragonese crossbowmen	Only from 1420	Light Foot	Unprotected	Average	Undrilled	Crossbow	–	5	6–8	0–12
Archers	Only from 1440	Light Foot	Unprotected	Average	Drilled	Bow	–	5	4–6	0–6
Turks	Only from 1440	Light Horse	Unprotected	Average	Undrilled	Bow	–	8	4–6	0–6
Albanian allies – See *Field of Glory Companion 6: Eternal Empire: The Ottomans at War.*										
Papal States										
Guardsmen		Heavy Foot	Protected	Superior	Drilled	–	Defensive Spearmen	9	4	0–4
English archers	Only before 1400	Medium Foot	Protected	Average	Drilled	Longbow	Swordsmen	9	4–8	0–8
Hungarians	Only before 1440	Light Horse	Unprotected	Average	Undrilled	Bow	–	8	4–6	0–6
Venice										
English archers	Only from 1400 to 1440	Medium Foot	Protected	Average	Drilled	Longbow	Swordsmen	9	4	0–4
Stakes to cover half the bases of longbow BG	Only from 1415	Portable defences						3		All or none
Archers	Only from 1440	Light Foot	Unprotected	Average	Drilled	Bow	–	5	4–6	0–6
Stradiots	Only from 1440	Light Horse	Unprotected	Average	Undrilled	Javelins	Light Spear, Swordsmen	9	4–6	In Italy 0–8, outside Italy 4–18
		Cavalry	Unprotected	Average	Undrilled	Javelins	Light Spear, Swordsmen	8		
			Protected					9		
Turks	Only from 1440	Light Horse	Unprotected	Average	Undrilled	Bow	–	8	4–6	0–6
Dalmatian men-at-arms (Only outside Italy)		Knights	Heavily Armoured	Superior	Undrilled	–	Lancers, Swordsmen	23	4	0–4
Swiss mercenary allies (Only in Italy from 1440)										0–16

MEDIEVAL CROWN OF ARAGON

This list covers the mainland armies of the Crown of Aragon from the coronation of Pere IV of Aragon (III of Catalonia) in 1336 until dynastic union with Castile in 1479. The Crown of Aragon ruled over a proto-federal state that reached its maximum expansion during this period. It included the Kingdom of Aragon, the Principality of Catalonia, the Kingdom of Majorca, the Kingdom of Valencia, the Kingdom of Sicily, Sardinia and the Kingdom of Naples, each one of them with its own independent political and juridical status. This list covers only its mainland armies.

French allies in 1365 represent Bertrand du Guesclin's White Companies, hired by Pere of Aragon for his war against Pedro of Castile. During the Catalan Civil War of 1462 to 1472 between King Juan II and the Catalan government of the Generalitat, French troops sent by Louis XI helped the king until 1466, when the Generalitat offered the Catalan crown to René d'Anjou and Louis XI changed sides.

TROOP NOTES

Aragonese men-at-arms rarely fought on foot. Drilled militia from the cities used pikes from the 13th century, but deep formations were not introduced until the arrival of foreign mercenaries in the second half of the 15th century. Almughavars were recruited from the border lands and are described as lightly armoured and equipped with a couple of iron darts, spear and short sword or dagger. Classification of their fighting style presents a problem – therefore we give a choice of classification. Their numbers and quality decreased as their main recruitment areas disappeared. A proportion of the army's spearmen, crossbowmen or archers can be Mudejars (Moslems) or Jews conscripted from the formerly Moslem areas.

Mudejar

MEDIEVAL CROWN OF ARAGON STARTER ARMY

Commander-in-Chief	1	Field Commander
Sub-commanders	2	2 x Troop Commander
Men-at-arms	2 BGs	Each comprising 4 bases of men-at-arms: Superior, Heavily Armoured, Undrilled Knights – Lancers, Swordsmen
Jinetes	1 BG	4 bases of jinetes: Average, Protected, Undrilled Light Horse – Javelins, Light Spear
Militia	2 BGs	Each comprising 6 bases of spearmen: Average, Protected, Drilled Heavy Foot – Offensive Spearmen
Crossbowmen	1 BG	8 bases of crossbowmen: Average, Protected, Drilled Medium Foot – Crossbow
Almughavars	2 BGs	Each comprising 6 bases of almughavars: Superior, Protected, Undrilled Medium Foot – Offensive Spearmen
Camp	1	Unfortified camp
Total	8 BGs	Camp, 12 mounted bases, 32 foot bases, 3 commanders

Aragonese light horseman and Castillian peasant levy, by Angus McBride. Taken from Men-at-Arms 200:
El Cid and the Reconquista 1050–1492.

BUILDING A CUSTOMISED LIST USING OUR ARMY POINTS

Choose an army based on the maxima and minima in the list below. The following special instructions apply to this army:

- Commanders should be depicted as men-at-arms.
- French or Free Company men-at-arms in 1365 (whether graded as Superior or Average when mounted) can always dismount as Superior, Heavily Armoured, Undrilled Heavy Foot – Heavy Weapon.
- In the Catalan Civil War of 1462 to 1472, French allies can be used only by royalist armies until 1466, and only by Generalitat armies thereafter.
- The minimum marked * does not apply to Generalitat armies, which can use only mercenary and French men-at-arms.
- The minima marked ** apply if any almughavars or almughavar skirmishers are used.
- All Medium Foot almughavars must be classified the same.
- The minima marked *** apply only if French or Free Company troops are used.
- A French allied commander can only command French or Free Company troops and must command all of them.

MEDIEVAL CROWN OF ARAGON

Territory Types: Agricultural, Developed, Hilly

C-in-C		Inspired Commander/Field Commander/Troop Commander						80/50/35		1	
Sub–commanders		Field Commander						50		0–2	
		Troop Commander						35		0–3	

Troop name		Troop Type				Capabilities		Points per base	Bases per BG	Total bases	
		Type	Armour	Quality	Training	Shooting	Close Combat				
Core Troops											
Feudal men-at-arms		Knights	Heavily Armoured	Superior	Undrilled	–	Lancers, Swordsmen	23	4–6	*4–16	
Mercenary men-at-arms	Only from 1410	Knights	Heavily Armoured	Average	Drilled	–	Lancers, Swordsmen	21	4–6	0–12	6–16
Military order men-at-arms		Knights	Heavily Armoured	Superior	Drilled	–	Lancers, Swordsmen	26	4	0–4	
Militia	Only before 1450	Heavy Foot	Protected	Average	Drilled	–	Offensive Spearmen	8	6–8	0–12	8–24
			Protected	Poor				6			
			Armoured	Average				10			
			Armoured	Poor				8			
	Only from 1450	Heavy Foot	Protected	Average	Drilled	–	Pikemen	6	8–12	0–12	
				Poor				4			
Other spearmen		Heavy Foot	Protected	Average	Undrilled	–	Defensive Spearmen	6	6–8	0–24	
				Poor				4			
Crossbowmen		Medium Foot	Protected	Average	Drilled	Crossbow	–	7	6–8	8–32	
					Undrilled			6			
		Light Foot	Unprotected	Average	Undrilled	Crossbow	–	5	6–8		
Optional Troops											
Jinetes or Adalides		Light Horse	Protected	Average	Undrilled	Javelins	Light Spear	8	4–6	0–8	
			Armoured					11			
Mounted crossbowmen		Light Horse	Protected	Average	Drilled	Crossbow	–	8	4	0–4	
			Armoured					11			
Military order crossbowmen		Medium Foot	Protected	Average	Drilled	Crossbow	–	7	4	0–4	

Almughavars	Before 1400	Medium Foot	Unprotected	Superior	Undrilled	–	Offensive Spearmen	7	6–8	**6–18
			Protected					9		
		Medium Foot	Unprotected	Superior	Undrilled	–	Impact Foot, Swordsmen	7	6–8	
			Protected					9		
	From 1400	Medium Foot	Unprotected	Average	Undrilled	–	Offensive Spearmen	6	6–8	**6–12
			Protected					7		
		Medium Foot	Unprotected	Average	Undrilled	–	Impact Foot, Swordsmen	6	6–8	
			Protected					7		
Almughavar skirmishers		Light Foot	Unprotected	Average	Undrilled	Javelins	Light Spear	4	4–6	0–6
Mercenary pikemen	Only from 1450	Heavy Foot	Protected	Average	Drilled	–	Pikemen	6	8	0–8
Archers		Light Foot	Unprotected	Average	Undrilled	Bow	–	5	4–6	0–6
				Poor				3		
Handgunners	Only from 1400	Light Foot	Unprotected	Average	Drilled	Firearm	–	4	4–8	0–8
			Protected					5		
Heavy guns		Heavy Artillery	–	Average	Undrilled	Heavy Artillery	–	20	2	0–2
French allied commander	Only in 1365 or from 1462 to 1472	Field Commander/Troop Commander						40/25		***1
French or Free Company men-at-arms		Knights	Heavily Armoured	Superior	Undrilled	–	Lancers, Swordsmen	23	4–6	****4–6
				Average				18		
French or Free Company crossbowmen		Medium Foot	Protected	Average	Undrilled	Crossbow	–	6	4–6	****4–6
Fortified camp								24		0–1

MEDIEVAL CROWN OF ARAGON ALLIES

Allied commander		Field Commander/Troop Commander						40/25		1
Troop name		**Troop Type**				**Capabilities**		Points per base	Bases per BG	Total bases
		Type	Armour	Quality	Training	Shooting	Close Combat			
Feudal men-at-arms		Knights	Heavily Armoured	Superior	Undrilled	–	Lancers, Swordsmen	23	4–6	4–6
Mercenary men-at-arms	Only from 1410	Knights	Heavily Armoured	Average	Drilled	–	Lancers, Swordsmen	21	4–6	
Jinetes or Adalides		Light Horse	Protected	Average	Undrilled	Javelins	Light Spear	8	4	0–4
			Armoured					11		
Militia	Only before 1450	Heavy Foot	Protected	Average	Drilled	–	Offensive Spearmen	8	4–8	4–8
			Protected	Poor				6		
			Armoured	Average				10		
			Armoured	Poor				8		
	Only from 1450	Heavy Foot	Protected	Average	Drilled	–	Pikemen	6	8	
				Poor				4		
Other spearmen		Heavy Foot	Protected	Average	Undrilled	–	Defensive Spearmen	6	4–8	
				Poor				4		
Crossbowmen		Medium Foot	Protected	Average	Drilled	Crossbow	–	7	4–8	4–8
					Undrilled			6		
		Light Foot	Unprotected	Average	Undrilled	Crossbow	–	5	4–8	
Almughavars	Before 1400	Medium Foot	Unprotected	Superior	Undrilled	–	Offensive Spearmen	7	4–6	0–6
			Protected					9		
		Medium Foot	Unprotected	Superior	Undrilled	–	Impact Foot, Swordsmen	7	4–6	
			Protected					9		
	From 1400	Medium Foot	Unprotected	Average	Undrilled	–	Offensive Spearmen	6	4	0–4
			Protected					7		
		Medium Foot	Unprotected	Average	Undrilled	–	Impact Foot, Swordsmen	6	4	
			Protected					7		

MEDIEVAL PORTUGESE

This list covers the armies of the kingdom of Portugal from the accession of Pedro I in 1357 until 1500. It covers Portuguese campaigns in Morocco.

Castilian allies represent Juana la Beltraneja's supporters during Alfonso V's intervention in the second Castilian civil war.

TROOP NOTES

Javelinmen were armed with javelins and a long thrusting spear. English and other Free Company men-at-arms in Spain usually fought on foot, and the Portuguese did also, at least during the latter 14th century.

PORTUGESE STARTER ARMY		
Commander-in-Chief	1	Field Commander
Sub-commanders	2	2 x Troop Commander
Men-at-arms	2 BGs	Each comprising 6 bases of men-at-arms: Average, Heavily Armoured, Undrilled Knights – Lancers, Swordsmen
Ginetes	1 BG	4 bases of ginetes: Average, Protected, Undrilled Light Horse – Javelins, Light Spear
Spearmen	1 BG	8 bases of spearmen: Average, Protected, Undrilled Heavy Foot –Defensive Spearmen
Archers	2 BGs	Each comprising 6 bases of archers: Average, Protected, Undrilled Medium Foot – Bow
Crossbowmen	1 BG	8 bases of crossbowmen: Average, Protected, Undrilled Medium Foot – Crossbow
Javelinmen	2 BGs	Each comprising 6 bases of javelinmen: Average, Unprotected, Undrilled Light Foot – Javelins, Light Spear
Camp	1	Unfortified camp
Total	9 BGs	Camp, 16 mounted bases, 40 foot bases, 3 commanders

BUILDING A CUSTOMISED LIST USING OUR ARMY POINTS

Choose an army based on the maxima and minima in the list below. The following special instructions apply to this army:

- Commanders should be depicted as men-at-arms.
- Portugese men-at-arms (whether graded as Superior or Average when mounted) can always dismount as Superior, Heavily Armoured, Undrilled Heavy Foot – Heavy Weapon.

- Military order men-at-arms can always dismount as Superior, Heavily Armoured, Drilled Heavy Foot – Heavy Weapon.
- The minimum marked * applies if more than one English or Free Company battle group is used. An English allied commander can only command English and/or Free Company troops, and, if used, must command all such troops.
- The minimum marked ** applies only if any English or Free Company troops are used.

MEDIEVAL PORTUGESE

Territory Types: Agricultural, Developed, Hilly

C-in-C		Inspired Commander/Field Commander/Troop Commander					80/50/35		1	
Sub-commanders		Field Commander					50		0–2	
		Troop Commander					35		0–3	
Troop name		Troop Type				Capabilities		Points per base	Bases per BG	Total bases
		Type	Armour	Quality	Training	Shooting	Impact			
Core Troops										
Portugese men-at-arms	Any date	Knights	Heavily Armoured	Superior	Undrilled	–	Lancers, Swordsmen	23	4–6	8–18
	Only from 1367 to 1390	Knights	Heavily Armoured	Average	Undrilled	–	Lancers, Swordsmen	18	4–6	8–18
Military order men-at-arms		Knights	Heavily Armoured	Superior	Drilled	–	Lancers, Swordsmen	26	4	0–4
Crossbowmen		Medium Foot	Protected	Average	Drilled	Crossbow	–	7	6–8	0–8
				Poor				5		
		Medium Foot	Protected	Average	Undrilled	Crossbow	–	6	6–8	0–32
				Poor				4		
		Light Foot	Unprotected	Average	Undrilled	Crossbow	–	5	6–8	8–48
				Poor				3		
Archers		Medium Foot	Protected	Average	Undrilled	Bow	–	6	6–8	0–32
			Protected	Poor				4		
			Unprotected	Average				5		
			Unprotected	Poor				3		
		Light Foot	Unprotected	Average	Undrilled	Bow	–	5	6–8	
				Poor				3		
Optional Troops										
Ginetes		Light Horse	Protected	Average	Undrilled	Javelins	Light Spear	8	4–6	0–6
			Armoured					11		
Mounted crossbowmen		Light Horse	Protected	Average	Drilled	Crossbow	–	8	4	0–4
			Armoured					11		
Military order crossbowmen		Medium Foot	Protected	Average	Drilled	Crossbow	–	7	4	0–4
Spearmen		Heavy Foot	Protected	Average	Drilled	–	Defensive Spearmen	7	6–8	0–8
				Poor				5		0–16
		Heavy Foot	Protected	Average	Undrilled	–	Defensive Spearmen	6	6–8	0–16
				Poor				4		
Javelinmen		Medium Foot	Protected	Average	Undrilled	–	Light Spear	5	6–8	0–32
			Protected	Poor				3		
			Unprotected	Average				4		
			Unprotected	Poor				2		
		Light Foot	Unprotected	Average	Undrilled	Javelins	Light Spear	4	6–8	
				Poor				2		
Handgunners	Only from 1400	Light Foot	Unprotected	Average	Drilled	Firearm	–	4	4–8	0–8
			Protected					5		
Heavy guns		Heavy Artillery	–	Average	Undrilled	Heavy Artillery	–	20	2	0–2

							Points	Bases per BG	Total
English allied commander	Field Commander/Troop Commander						40/25		*1
English or other Free Company men-at-arms	Heavy Foot	Heavily Armoured	Superior	Drilled	–	Heavy Weapon	16	4–6	0–8
Only from 1365 to 1390		Armoured	Superior	Drilled			13		
		Armoured	Average	Drilled			10		
		Heavily Armoured	Superior	Undrilled			14		
English longbowmen	Medium Foot	Protected	Average	Drilled	Longbow	Swordsmen	9	4–8	**4–8
Free Company crossbowmen	Medium Foot	Protected	Average	Undrilled	Crossbow	–	6	4–6	0–6
Field defences – abatis or trenches	Field Fortifications						3		0–20
Fortified camp							24		0–1
Allies									
Castilian allies (Only 1474 to 1476) – Medieval Castilian									

MEDIEVAL CASTILIAN

This list covers the armies of the kingdom of Castile from the accession of Pedro I the Cruel in 1350 until the reform of the army and the creation of the Santa Hermandad Nueva by Ferdinand and Isabella in 1476.

TROOP NOTES

Castilian men-at-arms rarely fought on foot, though the Order of the Sash accompanied the French dismounted knights at Najera (1367). French and Free Company men-at-arms in Spain usually fought on foot. A proportion of the spearmen, crossbowmen, archers or javelinmen can be Mudejars (Moslems) or Jews conscripted from the formerly Moslem areas. Javelinmen were armed with javelins and a long thrusting spear. A Castilian ordinance of 1385 specifies spear, javelin and shield as the required equipment for those with an income of 400–600 maravedis, and spear and javelin for those in the lowest bracket of less than 400 maravedis. Those with an income of 600–2,000 maravedis were to muster as crossbowmen, those with 2,000–3,000 maravedis as spearmen with helmet, shield, spear and sword.

MEDIEVAL CASTILIAN STARTER ARMY		
Commander-in-Chief	1	Field Commander
Sub-commanders	2	2 x Troop Commander
Men-at-arms	3 BGs	Each comprising 4 bases of men-at-arms: Superior, Heavily Armoured, Undrilled Knights – Lancers, Swordsmen
Jinetes	2 BGs	Each comprising 4 bases of jinetes: Average, Protected, Undrilled Light Horse – Javelins, Light Spear
Spearmen	2 BGs	Each comprising 6 bases of spearmen: Average, Protected, Undrilled Heavy Foot – Defensive Spearmen
Crossbowmen	2 BGs	Each comprising 6 bases of crossbowmen: Average, Unprotected, Undrilled Light Foot – Crossbow
Camp	1	Unfortified camp
Total	9 BGs	Camp, 20 mounted bases, 24 foot bases, 3 commanders

BUILDING A CUSTOMISED LIST USING OUR ARMY POINTS

Choose an army based on the maxima and minima in the list below. The following special instructions apply to this army:

- Commanders should be depicted as men-at-arms.
- French or Free Company men-at-arms (whether graded as Superior or Average when mounted) can always dismount as Superior, Heavily Armoured, Undrilled Heavy Foot – Heavy Weapon.
- Military order men-at-arms can always dismount as Superior, Heavily Armoured, Drilled Heavy Foot – Heavy Weapon.
- The minima marked * apply if any French, Free Company or Navarrese troops are used.

- A French allied commander can only command French or Free Company troops and must command all of them.
- A Navarrese allied commander can only command Navarrese troops and must command all of them.

Granadine Cavalry

Aragonese knight and Castillian crossbowman, by Angus McBride. Taken from Men-at-Arms 200: El Cid and the Reconquista 1050–1492.

MEDIEVAL CASTILIAN

Territory Types: Agricultural, Developed, Hilly

Troop name		Troop Type				Capabilities		Points per base	Bases per BG	Total bases	
		Type	Armour	Quality	Training	Shooting	Close Combat				
C-in-C		Inspired Commander/Field Commander/Troop Commander						80/50/35		1	
Sub-commanders		Field Commander						50		0–2	
		Troop Commander						35		0–3	
Core Troops											
Men-at-arms		Knights	Heavily Armoured	Superior	Undrilled	–	Lancers, Swordsmen	23	4–6	8–20	8–20
Military order men-at-arms		Knights	Heavily Armoured	Superior	Drilled	–	Lancers, Swordsmen	26	4	0–4	
Jinetes		Light Horse	Protected	Average	Undrilled	Javelins	Light Spear	8	4–6	4–12	
			Armoured					11			
Crossbowmen		Medium Foot	Protected	Average	Undrilled	Crossbow	–	6	6–8	8–24	
				Average	Drilled			7			
				Poor	Undrilled			4			
				Poor	Drilled			5			
		Light Foot	Unprotected	Average	Undrilled	Crossbow	–	5	6–8		
				Poor				3			
Optional Troops											
Mounted crossbowmen		Light Horse	Protected	Average	Drilled	Crossbow	–	8	4	0–4	
			Armoured					11			
Granadine cavalry		Light Horse	Unprotected	Average	Drilled	Javelins	Light Spear	7	4	0–4	
Hermandad or military order spearmen		Heavy Foot	Protected	Average	Drilled	–	Defensive Spearmen	7	6–8	0–8	0–16
			Protected	Poor				5			
			Armoured	Average				9			
			Armoured	Poor				7			
Other spearmen		Heavy Foot	Protected	Average	Undrilled	–	Defensive Spearmen	6	6–8	0–16	
				Poor				4			
Military order crossbowmen		Medium Foot	Protected	Average	Drilled	Crossbow	–	7	4	0–4	
Javelinmen		Medium Foot	Protected	Average	Undrilled	–	Light Spear	5	6–8	0–12	
			Protected	Poor				3			
			Unprotected	Average				4			
			nprotected	Poor				2			
		Light Foot	Unprotected	Average	Undrilled	Javelins	Light Spear	4	6–8		
				Poor				2			
Archers		Medium Foot	Protected	Average	Undrilled	Bow	–	6	6–8	0–8	
			Protected	Poor				4			
			Unprotected	Average				5			
			Unprotected	Poor				3			
		Light Foot	Unprotected	Average	Undrilled	Bow	–	5	6–8		
				Poor				3			
Slingers		Light Foot	Unprotected	Average	Undrilled	Sling	–	4	6–8	0–12	
				Poor				2			
Handgunners	Only from 1400	Light Foot	Unprotected	Average	Drilled	Firearm	–	4	4–8	0–8	
			Protected					5			
Heavy guns		Heavy Artillery	–	Average	Undrilled	Heavy Artillery	–	20	2	0–2	
French or Navarrese ally commander		Field Commander/Troop Commander						40/25		*1	
French, Free Company or Navarrese men-at-arms	French or Free Company only before 1390, Navarrese only from 1410	Knights	Heavily Armoured	Superior	Undrilled	–	Lancers, Swordsmen	23	4–6	*4–6	
				Average				18			
French, Free Company or Navarrese crossbowmen		Medium Foot	Protected	Average	Undrilled	Crossbow	–	6	4–6	0–6	
Navarrese javelinmen		Medium Foot	Protected	Average	Undrilled	–	Light Spear	5	4–6	0–6	
			Unprotected					4			
		Light Foot	Unprotected	Average	Undrilled	Javelins	Light Spear	4	4–6		
Fortified camp								24		0–1	
Allies											
Aragonese allies (Only from 1410 to 1476) – Medieval Crown of Aragon											

MEDIEVAL CASTILIAN ALLIES

Allied commander	Field Commander/Troop Commander						40/25		1	
Troop name	Troop Type				Capabilities		Points per base	Bases per BG	Total bases	
	Type	Armour	Quality	Training	Shooting	Close Combat				
Men-at-arms	Knights	Heavily Armoured	Superior	Undrilled	–	Lancers, Swordsmen	23	4–6	4–8	
Jinetes	Light Horse	Protected	Average	Undrilled	Javelins	Light Spear	8	4	4	
		Armoured					11			
Crossbowmen	Medium Foot	Protected	Average	Undrilled	Crossbow	–	6	4–8	4–8	
			Average	Drilled			7			
			Poor	Undrilled			4			
			Poor	Drilled			5			
	Light Foot	Unprotected	Average	Undrilled	Crossbow	–	5	4–8		
			Poor				3			
Hermandad or military order spearmen	Heavy Foot	Protected	Average	Drilled	–	Defensive Spearmen	7	4	0–4	0–6
		Protected	Poor				5			
		Armoured	Average				9			
		Armoured	Poor				7			
Other spearmen	Heavy Foot	Protected	Average	Undrilled	–	Defensive Spearmen	6	4–6	0–6	
			Poor				4			
Javelinmen	Medium Foot	Protected	Average	Undrilled	–	Light Spear	5	4		0–4
		Protected	Poor				3			
		Unprotected	Average				4			
		Unprotected	Poor				2			
	Light Foot	Unprotected	Average	Undrilled	Javelins	Light Spear	4	4		
			Poor				2			
Slingers	Light Foot	Unprotected	Average	Undrilled	Sling	–	4	4		
			Poor				2			

SANTA HERMANDAD NUEVA CASTILIAN

This list covers the armies of Castile from the creation of the Santa Hermandad Nueva in 1476 until its disappearance with the ordinance of 1497, which for the first time reorganized the infantry into thirds of differently equipped troops, starting a series of reforms that would end up with the Tercios that began modern warfare. This was the army that finally conquered Granada, the last Moslem state in Spain, in 1492.

TROOP NOTES

Infantry became more and more important, accounting for up to $5/6$ of the army that finally took Granada. In parallel, the number of men-at-arms was reduced in favour of extra

light cavalry, and by the end of the war there were up to ten times as many jinetes as heavy cavalry. The ordinance of 1488 organized the Santa Hermandad Nueva into 12 companies of 720 spearmen and 80 arquebusiers, plus 24 officers, 8 drummers and a standard-bearer. Some of those companies were equipped with pikes instead of spears, and operated in the manner of the Swiss and Germans. Other Hermandades had equal numbers of spearmen and crossbowmen, and sword-and-buckler men were used specially for assaults during sieges. The military orders were still present in the War of Granada; the master of the Order of Calatrava was killed at Loja in 1482, and the master of

the Order of Santiago commanded the rearguard of the army that had to withdraw from the mountains of Malaga in 1483. Other troops included almughavars and Swiss mercenaries. Classification of the fighting style of almughavars presents a problem – therefore we give a choice of classification. The artillery train was a very important part of the army and played a decisive role in the different sieges that took place over the War of Granada.

Troop Commander

SANTA HERMANDAD NUEVA CASTILIAN STARTER ARMY

Commander-in-Chief	1	Field Commander
Sub-commanders	2	2 x Troop Commander
Men-at-arms	1 BG	4 bases of men-at-arms: Superior, Heavily Armoured, Undrilled Knights – Lancers, Swordsmen
Jinetes	2 BGs	Each comprising 4 bases of jinetes: Average, Protected, Undrilled Light Horse – Javelins, Light Spear
Santa Hermandad Nueva pikemen	1 BG	8 bases of pikemen: Average, Protected, Drilled Heavy Foot – Pikemen
Santa Hermandad Nueva spearmen	2 BGs	Each comprising 4 bases of spearmen: Average, Armoured, Drilled Heavy Foot – Offensive Spearmen
Other Hermandad spearmen	1 BG	6 bases of spearmen: Average, Protected, Drilled Heavy Foot – Defensive Spearmen
Hermandad arquebusiers	1 BG	6 bases of arquebusiers: Average, Protected, Drilled Light Foot - Firearm
Hermandad crossbowmen	1 BG	6 bases of crossbowmen: Average, Protected, Drilled Medium Foot – Crossbow
Hermandad sword and buckler men	1 BG	6 bases of sword and buckler men: Superior, Armoured, Drilled Medium Foot – Skilled Swordsmen
Camp	1	Unfortified camp
Total	10 BGs	Camp, 12 mounted bases, 40 foot bases, 3 commanders

BUILDING A CUSTOMISED LIST USING OUR ARMY POINTS

Choose an army based on the maxima and minima in the list below. The following special instructions apply to this army:

- Commanders should be depicted as men-at-arms.
- All Medium Foot almughavars must be classified the same.

SANTA HERMANDAD NUEVA CASTILIAN

Territory Types: Agricultural, Developed, Hilly

C-in-C		Inspired Commander/Field Commander/Troop Commander					80/50/35		1	
Sub-commanders		Field Commander					50		0–2	
		Troop Commander					35		0–3	
Troop name		**Troop Type**				**Capabilities**		**Points per base**	**Bases per BG**	**Total bases**
		Type	Armour	Quality	Training	Shooting	Close Combat			
Core Troops										
Men-at-arms		Knights	Heavily Armoured	Superior	Undrilled	–	Lancers, Swordsmen	23	4–6	0–10
Military order men-at-arms		Knights	Heavily Armoured	Superior	Drilled	–	Lancers, Swordsmen	26	4	0–4	0–10
Jinetes		Light Horse	Protected	Average	Undrilled	Javelins	Light Spear	8	4–6	8–20
			Armoured					11		
Santa Hermandad Nueva spearmen		Heavy Foot	Protected	Average	Drilled	–	Offensive Spearmen	8	4–8	6–20
			Armoured					10			6–20
Santa Hermandad Nueva pikemen		Heavy Foot	Protected	Average	Drilled	–	Pikemen	6	8–12	0–12
Other Hermandad spearmen		Heavy Foot	Protected	Average	Drilled	–	Defensive Spearmen	7	4–8	6–20	6–20
			Armoured					9		
Hermandad sword and buckler men		Medium foot	Protected	Superior	Drilled	–	Skilled swordsmen	10	4–8	0–8
			Armoured					13		
Hermandad crossbowmen		Medium Foot	Protected	Average	Drilled	Crossbow	–	7	4–8	4–20	8–20
Hermandad arquebusiers		Light Foot	Unprotected	Average	Drilled	Firearm	–	4	4–8	0–12
			Protected					5		
Optional Troops										
Mounted crossbowmen		Light Horse	Protected	Average	Drilled	Crossbow	–	8	4	0–4
			Armoured					11		
Military order crossbowmen		Medium Foot	Protected	Average	Drilled	Crossbow	–	7	4	0–4
Other spearmen		Heavy Foot	Protected	Poor	Undrilled	–	Defensive Spearmen	4	6–8	0–8
Other crossbowmen		Medium Foot	Protected	Poor	Undrilled	Crossbow	–	4	6–8	0–8
		Light Foot	Unprotected	Average	Undrilled	Crossbow	–	5	6–8	
				Poor				3		
Other archers		Medium Foot	Protected	Poor	Undrilled	Bow	–	4	6–8	
		Light Foot	Unprotected	Average	Undrilled	Bow	–	5	6–8	
				Poor				3		
Almughavars and adalides		Medium Foot	Unprotected	Average	Undrilled	–	Offensive Spearmen	6	6–8	0–8
			Protected					7		
		Medium Foot	Unprotected	Average	Undrilled	–	Impact Foot, Swordsmen	6	6–8	
			Protected					7		
		Light Foot	Unprotected	Average	Undrilled	Javelins	Light Spear	4	4–6	
Heavy guns		Heavy Artillery	–	Average	Undrilled	Heavy Artillery	–	20	2	0–4
Swiss mercenaries	Only after 1482	Heavy Foot	Protected	Superior	Drilled	–	Pikemen	8	8	0–8
Field Fortifications		Field Fortifications						3		0–16
Fortified camp								24		0–1

LATER GRANADINE

The Kingdom of Granada was the last surviving remnant of Moslem rule in the Iberian peninsula. This list covers Granadine armies from 1340 until the fall of the kingdom in 1492. Ruled by the Nasrid dysnasty, Granada was a major entrepôt for trade with North and Sub-Saharan Africa, particularly the gold trade. Granada was rich and

heavily populated. Its borders were mountainous and protected by a chain of fortresses.

TROOP NOTES

Most mercenary foot were Black Africans from Sub-Saharan Africa or Berbers from North Africa.

LATER GRANADINE STARTER ARMY

Commander-in-Chief	1	Field Commander
Sub-commanders	2	2 x Troop Commander
Lancers	2 BGs	Each comprising 4 bases of lancers: Superior, Armoured, Drilled Cavalry – Lancers, Swordsmen
Light Horse	3 BGs	Each comprising 6 bases of light horse: Average, Unprotected, Drilled Light Horse – Javelins, Light Spear
Spearmen	2 BGs	Each comprising 6 bases of spearmen: Average, Protected, Drilled Heavy Foot – Defensive Spearmen
Crossbowmen	3 BGs	Each comprising 8 bases of crossbowmen: Average, Unprotected, Undrilled Light Foot – Crossbow
Camp	1	Unfortified camp
Total	10 BGs	Camp, 26 mounted bases, 36 foot bases, 3 commanders

BUILDING A CUSTOMISED LIST USING OUR ARMY POINTS

Choose an army based on the maxima and minima in the list below. The following special

instructions apply to this army:

• Commanders should be depicted as lancers.

LATER GRANADINE

Territory Types: Mountains

Troop name	Troop Type				Capabilities		Points per base	Bases per BG	Total bases
	Type	Armour	Quality	Training	Shooting	Close Combat			
C-in-C	Inspired Commander/Field Commander/Troop Commander						80/50/35	1	
Sub-commanders	Field Commander						50	0–2	
	Troop Commander						35	0–3	
Core Troops									
Lancers	Cavalry	Armoured	Superior	Drilled	–	Lancers, Swordsmen	17	4–6	4–8
Light horse	Light Horse	Unprotected	Average	Drilled	Javelins	Light Spear	7	4–6	8–30
Mounted crossbowmen	Light Horse	Unprotected	Average	Drilled	Crossbow	–	7	4–6	0–6
Peasant crossbowmen	Light Foot	Unprotected	Average	Undrilled	Crossbow	–	5	6–8	16–96
			Poor				3		
	Medium Foot	Unprotected	Average	Undrilled	Crossbow	–	5	6–8	
			Poor				3		

Optional Troops									
Christian mercenary men-at-arms	Knights	Heavily armoured	Superior	Undrilled	–	Lancers, Swordsmen	23	4	0–4
Mercenary or town militia spearmen	Heavy Foot	Protected	Average	Drilled	–	Defensive Spearmen	7	6–8	0–12
			Poor				5		
Mercenary or town militia crossbowmen	Medium Foot	Protected	Average	Drilled	Crossbow	–	7	4–6	0–8
			Poor				5		
Mercenary archers	Medium Foot	Protected	Average	Drilled	Bow	–	7	4–6	
Handgunners	Only from 1450	Light Foot	Unprotected	Average	Drilled	Firearm	–	4	4–6	0–6
Slingers		Light Foot	Unprotected	Average	Undrilled	Sling	–	4	4–6	0–6
Fortified camp								24		0–1

APPENDIX 1 – USING THE LISTS

To give balanced games, armies can be selected using the points system. The more effective the troops, the more each base costs in points. The maximum points for an army will usually be set at between 600 and 800 points for a singles game for 2 to 4 hours play. We recommend 800 points for 15mm singles tournament games (650 points for 25mm) and 1000 points for 15mm doubles games.

The army lists specify which troops can be used in a particular army. No other troops can be used. The number of bases of each type in the army must conform to the specified minima and maxima. Troops that have restrictions on when they can be used cannot be used with troops with a conflicting restriction. For example, troops that can only be used "before 1450" cannot be used with troops that can only be used "from 1450". All special instructions applying to an army list must be adhered to. They also apply to allied contingents supplied by the army.

All armies must have a C-in-C and at least one other commander. No army can have more than 4 commanders in total, including C-in-C, sub-commanders and allied commanders.

All armies must have a supply camp. This is free unless fortified. A fortified camp can only be used if specified in the army list. Field fortifications and portable defences can only be used if specified in the army list.

Allied contingents can only be used if specified in the army list. Most allied contingents have their own allied contingent list, to which they must conform unless the main army's list specifies otherwise.

BATTLE GROUPS

All troops are organized into battle groups. Commanders, supply camps and field fortifications are not troops and are not assigned to battle groups. Portable defences are not troops, but are assigned to specific battle groups.

Battle groups must obey the following restrictions:

- The number of bases in a battle group must correspond to the range specified in the army list.
- Each battle group must initially comprise an even number of bases. The only exception to this rule is that battle groups whose army list specifies them as $2/3$ of one type and $1/3$ of another, can comprise 9 bases if this is within the battle group size range specified by the list.

- A battle group can only include troops from one line in a list, unless the list specifies a mixed formation by specifying fractions of the battle group to be of types from two lines. e.g. $^2/_3$ spearmen, $^1/_3$ archers.
- All troops in a battle group must be of the same quality and training. When a choice of quality or training is given in a list, this allows battle groups to differ from each other. It does not permit variety within a battle group.
- Unless specifically stated otherwise in an army list, all troops in a battle group must be of the same armour class. When a choice of armour class is given in a list, this allows battle groups to differ from each other. It does not permit variety within a battle group.

EXAMPLE LIST

Here is a section of an actual army list, which will help us to explain the basics and some special features. The list specifies the following items for each historical type included in the army:

- Troop Type – comprising Type, Armour, Quality and Training..
- Capabilities – comprising Shooting and Close Combat capabilities..
- Points cost per base.
- Minimum and maximum number of bases in each battle group.

- Minimum and maximum number of bases in the army.

Special features:

- Feudal men-at-arms can be Superior or Average. The list specifies the different points costs. All the bases in a battle group must be of the same quality. The army must include between 4 and 16 bases of feudal men-at-arms, organized into battle groups of from 4 to 6 bases each.
- Select levy can be Drilled or Undrilled. All the bases in a battle group must be of the same training. A select levy battle group can either have all of its bases as heavy foot with heavy weapon, or half of its bases as heavy foot with heavy weapon and half as medium foot with crossbow. Each battle group must have from 6 to 8 bases in total. The army must include between 12 and 24 bases of select levy.
- Separately deployed mounted attendants can be Average or Poor. All the bases in a battle group must be of the same quality. The army is allowed from 0–4 bases i.e. 1 battle group.
- Mounted Handgunners can only be used from 1450. The army is allowed from 0–4 bases i.e. 1 battle group.
- The total number of bases of mounted attendants, mounted crossbowmen and mounted Handgunners in the army cannot exceed 8.

Troop name	Troop Type				Capabilities		Points per base	Bases per BG	Total bases	
	Type	Armour	Quality	Training	Shooting	Close Combat				
Feudal men-at-arms	Knights	Heavily Armoured	Superior	Undrilled	–	Lancers, Swordsmen	23	4–6	4–16	
			Average				18			
Select levy	Heavy Foot	Armoured	Average	Drilled	–	Heavy Weapon	10	1/2 or all	12–24	
				Undrilled			9			
	Medium Foot	Armoured	Average	Drilled	Crossbow	Swordsmen	10	1/2 or none	6–8	
				Undrilled			9			
Separately deployed mounted attendants	Cavalry	Protected	Average	Undrilled	–	Swordsmen	8	4	0–4	
			Poor				6			
Mounted crossbowmen	Cavalry	Armoured	Average	Undrilled	Crossbow	Swordsmen	13	4–6	0–8	0–8
Mounted handgunners	Only from 1450	Cavalry	Armoured	Average	Undrilled	Firearm	Swordsmen	12	4	0–4

APPENDIX 2 – THEMED TOURNAMENTS

A tournament based on the "Storm of Arrows" theme can include any of the armies listed in this book.

INDEX